BREAKING THE BARRIER OF AVERAGE

BY RON KUTINSKY

Breaking the Barrier of Average

By Ron Kutinsky
Published by
Blaze Publishing House
BlazePublishingHouse.com
Mansfield, TX

Unless otherwise noted, all Scripture taken from the New King James Version®. Copyright © 1982 by Thomas Nelson. Used by permission. All rights reserved.

Scripture quotations taken from the The Holy Bible, New International Version® NIV® Copyright © 1973, 1978, 1984, 2011 by Biblica, Inc.® Used by permission. All rights reserved worldwide.

Scripture quotations taken from the The Message (MSG). Copyright © 1993, 1994, 1995, 1996, 2000, 2001, 2002. Used by permission of NavPress Publishing Group.

Scripture quotations taken from the Amplified® Bible (AMPC), Copyright © 1954, 1958, 1962, 1964, 1965, 1987 by The Lockman Foundation. Used by permission. www.Lockman.org

Scripture quotations taken from The ESV® Bible, The Holy Bible, English Standard Version®. Copyright © 2001 by Crossway, a publishing ministry of Good News Publishers. The ESV® text has been reproduced in cooperation with and by permission of Good News Publishers. Unauthorized reproduction of this publication is prohibited. All rights reserved.

Manuscript development – Kent Booth

ISBN 13: 978-0-9968803-5-0

Printed Version

Copyright © 2017 Ron Kutinsky

All rights reserved.

WHAT "AVERAGE BUSTERS" ARE SAYING

YOU DON'T HAVE to be around Ron and Donna Kutinsky very long to figure out they live what they believe, preach, and put in print. While the Church today is quick to squelch creative thinking, dreaming, and prophetic vision, they can't hold Ron down. He just steps up and writes an incredibly creative, prophetic book. *Breaking the Barrier of Average* walks you through the process of changing the way you think regarding dreaming and living. As Ron points out, the real joy of discovering your dream and destiny is bringing others with you on the journey. Ron does just that. His insights from his own journey will help you navigate through the exciting maze of freedom. Get ready to dream big with a big God who delights in your adventures just as much as you do.

PS: Look for the B.B.'s. They're awesome!

Ms. Button Wright
Founder and President, 4:11 Ministries, Corp

Average! Average! None of my children are average! What's he talking about? But to tell the truth, even the best of us sometimes sink to "average" or below at certain times or in certain areas. This book is an elegant and available ladder to help us climb up, with the help of the Lord. We can emerge into the sunshine and a life well worth living. I'm proud to call the author my son.

Eileen Kutinsky
CEO Shinn Farms, missionary, teacher (ret.)

Have you settled for a mediocre, ordinary, garden variety, dime-a-dozen, run-of-the-mill, tolerable, unexceptional life? Are you treading water, about to drown in a commonplace pond, instead of reaching the shore of outstanding.? Then your greatest enemy is "average." It's time to break through that barrier into a life of significance.

In this marvelous, practical book, Ron Kutinsky declares that the dream your heart is achievable. Like an inner compass, it unlocks your passion and purpose. *Breaking the Barrier of Average* is a how-to book that guides you from the figment of your dream to the reality of its fulfillment. Don't settle for normal. Be exceptional!

Ron is a dear friend whose words of encouragement and wisdom have not only blessed my life but countless others. His nuggets of wisdom are truly barrier-breakers which will propel you into achieving your dream life—one that is blessed to be a blessing to others.

I highly recommend this book.

Dr. Dale A. Fife
Founder and President, Mountain Top Global Ministries.
Author of *The Secret Place, Passionately Pursuing God's Presence.*

Ron Kutinsky's book, *Breaking the Barrier of Average*, is an example of what the title means. This is not an "average" book. By giving concrete ways on how to achieve your destiny, Ron skillfully displays how to break out of settling for anything less than what God designed you to be. I love the descriptive and prescriptive nature of this book. Ron, thanks for not settling for "average!"

Dale Schlafer
Center for World Revival and Awakening
Bradenton, Florida

Breaking the Barrier of Average is not a book of clichés and cute sayings, it is a way of life for Ron Kutinsky. He is a master at extracting practical and powerful how-to's from his own journey and putting them in a format that is easy to digest. Each chapter is rich with actionable strategies that you can implement immediately. This is not a book you'll read once, but it's a manual for success you'll reference forever. No fluff here, just concise, clear strategies you use today to create the life you've always wanted.

Dennis McIntee
Author of numerous books including *The 8 Qualities of Drama Free Teams*

Reading *Breaking the Barrier of Average* is like soaking in a refreshing conversation with a seasoned man who is handing you precious keys for next level living. Ron Kutinsky is that man. In every chapter, he upgrades your thinking to produce powerful fruit in your life. If you want to be equipped and encouraged to keep climbing higher this book is for you.

Mark DeJesus
Author & Transformational Consultant

ACKNOWLEDGEMENTS

FIRST OF ALL, I would like to thank God who has saved me, loved me, taught me, called me and encouraged me. And who, like His disciples, has called me His friend.

I would like to express my love and gratitude to my life-long best friend, my inspiration, my lover, and my wife, Donna Kutinsky. Not only is she my life-partner, she has also mentored me in many breaking the barrier of "average" ways. There's no one on the planet that I would rather be journeying this adventurous life with than you! I love you, Donna, now and forever.

To my two beautiful daughters, Colleen and Jenelle. Oh, how I wish I had known all the things in this book when you were young. I've often wondered why God gives us children when we're young and so void of knowledge. What an honor it is to now be able to share these truths with you and the energy-packs known as our grandkids!

Also, a huge thank you to the precious people who supported this book: Adam and Donna Hernandez, Eileen Kutinsky, Tina Miccio, Brett and Angela Muncie, and Jack and Jackie Shapiro.

To my Mother, Eileen Kutinsky. You by far are one of the most inspiring "Average Busters" I know. Thank you for your love, your amazing support, and your numerous average breaking examples.

To my Dad, now ninety years young, and who honors me and humbles me by sitting under my teaching every week taking notes! You have a heart the size of Texas. Thank you for your love and support.

To the greatest congregation this side of Heaven: Hope International Ministries. I love my H.I.M. family! Thanks for your love, support, and inspiration.

To Kent Booth and Blaze Publishing. Thank you for your friendship and for your diligence, patience, and expertise working with me on this project. I look forward to working with you on future books.

TABLE OF CONTENTS

CHAPTER 1

TEACH ME TO SWIM

IT WAS THE summer of my high school junior year. What started out as a typical, innocent Ohio summer day ended in a way that changed my life forever.

For the previous two years, I worked as the lone lifeguard at a campground just outside Streetsboro, Ohio. After that time the campground hired another lifeguard which freed me to do other tasks like maintenance and even some office work. One of my duties was to train the new lifeguard, which meant informing him of a risky practice the kids often attempted.

The campground housed a beautiful five-acre lake. Even though it looked inviting on the surface, what lay underneath could be quite dangerous. The lake had a great sandy bottom but with a gradual drop-off that was quite tricky to navigate. No matter how many times the kids—and their parents—were lectured, threatened, and even temporarily banned from the lake, the kids still participated in a very dangerous activity…one that beckoned me to their rescue more than once.

Many of these kids couldn't even swim, but the lure of the deep kept calling. Their curiosity led them out as deep as they could go. But that wasn't enough. With the water cresting around their neck, they ventured out even deeper. Standing on their tip-toes, these young adventurers would tilt their heads back and continue on until only their lips protruded out of the water. It was in this precarious position that many lost their balance and required rescuing.

Only on this day, rescue didn't come in time.

Did the murky water hide him? Maybe the lifeguard wasn't as attentive as he needed to be. Whatever the case, I watched in shocked horror as a little eight-year-old boy's life cruelly and permanently drained away. What would he have grown up to be? A doctor, a fireman, an accountant? How many lives would he have impacted? Would he have married? Had kids of his own? I wrestled with the reality that these questions would never be answered.

Now, you're probably thinking, *Wow. What a sad way to start a book!* And I agree, it is. But keep reading. The point and parallel of this story paint the purpose of this entire book.

ONE STEP AWAY

As the paramedic's life-saving efforts halted and this little boy's struggle to live ended, something hit me like a ton of bricks: how easily this tragedy could have been averted. The more I dwelt on it, what irked me the most was how no one ever taught this boy to swim! He walked into an environment that eventually sucked the life out of him—*without any preparation*. If his parents would have only known the impending dangers he faced, I'm sure they would have spared no expense for proper training.

But they didn't.

And his young life tragically ended.

Here's the parallel: Today, we have great institutions of learning where kids attend twelve and a half years. Then, four-plus years of college. Along the way, we as parents teach them many things, just as our parents taught us. Finally, graduation comes and they're launched out into the world—the environment waiting to suck the life out of them. But there's a problem. Even with all the education...

...They are *not prepared.*

It never ceases to amaze me how many people I've met, and even counseled, who are just like these kids in the lake. They are standing on their tiptoes with their lips barely above the water line, barely surviving. These people are everywhere! Thankfully, I've been blessed to rescue some, but sadly, many have gone under. Why? The exact same reason: They're not prepared for life.

Allow me to ask you a very honest question, which will require a very honest answer. Are you one of these people? Does this scenario describe your life? Maybe you're married to or parenting someone like this. Do you have a co-worker who's one step away from drowning? If so, that's okay. It may be the reason you bought this book!

Perhaps you're on the other end of the spectrum and your life is in good shape. That's awesome. But, let me remind you of those kids. Right up to the point of losing their balance and slipping below the water, they thought they were in a pretty good spot, too. What started out as having fun by enjoying the lake on a hot summer's day, turned into tragedy with just one step. Now, the real question:

Are you one step away from disaster?

To find out, take a look at a few diagnostic questions.

- If you lost your income, how long would it be before you filed for bankruptcy? (For the average American, it's about forty-five days.)

- In living your current lifestyle of diet and exercise, how many days premature will you die? (For most Americans it's not days or months, but years.)

- How about your relationships? Are they functioning at their minimum capacity, maximum capacity, or somewhere in between?

- If you took advantage of all your "should've, could've, and would've" in life, where would you be today?

- Are you living to your fullest potential, making your largest impact on your family, work environment, and society?

- Are you angry that, at your age, you're just now climbing out on dry land to be a lifeguard to others?

- Are you laying on the beach of life, short of breath but alive, screaming, *Why didn't anyone teach me to swim?*

If you're finding yourself in one or more of these, I have good news for you: This book is for you! It's designed to teach you how to successfully navigate through life's perilous waters.

You may even find yourself asking, *Why didn't they teach me this in school?* My prayer is that as you read, you ask many questions. Keep asking, and you will find the answers.

Throughout the pages of this book, you will find highlighted nuggets of information labeled B.B.: "Barrier Breakers." These are power phrases that will help you in your journey to greatness. Here's the first one:

> B.B.: Questions grant you access to the information library of life.

So, are you ready to stop drowning? Good.
Get ready to learn how to swim!

CHAPTER 2

KNOW YOUR ENEMY

WHEN SETTING OUT to find a restaurant, do you look for an "average" one? You know, one that serves average food, has average service, and boasts an average atmosphere. Of course you don't. Why? Because just like the Israelites were meant to taste the fruits of the Promised Land, you're built to taste the grapes! And "average" just won't cut it.

Let's shift from restaurants to life. Yes, daily manna is good, but there's more for you to taste. I'm not talking about always having the best of the best. In fact, true Kingdom living will self-sacrifice for others. Maybe you don't have the best because you're too busy *being* the best for yourself and others. The life I'm talking about is one that doesn't settle for mediocre, apathetic, or mundane living.

Once you became a child of God, your spiritual DNA completely changed. Your DNA is now God's DNA. And who is God? He is a king. Not just any king. In fact, the Bible calls

Him the "King of kings and Lord of lords!" (See 1 Timothy 6:15, Revelation 17:14, Revelation 19:16.) With that thought in mind, it's easy to see why you should never settle for anything less than what's already in you, right? However, if you're living far beneath that privilege, then you must ask, "Why?" The answer is quite simple:

You have a stealthy enemy sent straight from hell!

This enemy isn't like most. It's not designed to kill you directly. Instead, it flies unnoticed under the radar screen of your life, sabotaging your motivation, causing you to slip quietly below the surface and die. Like carbon monoxide, its works are undetected by its victims. Not only is it lethal and stealthy, this enemy is everywhere. What is it? I'm glad you asked.

It's the enemy called "average!"

BREAK IT DOWN

"Average" can be found in every phase and stage of life. For example, it's designed to turn:

- sleeping with the wife/husband of your youth into sleeping with a roommate.

- your living room into your "dying" room.

- your dreams into a mere job.

- your ministry opportunity into nap time.

- your marriage into maintenance.

- your preparation for greatness into Preparation H, (Ho-Hum).

- your destiny into distraction.

When it comes down to it, defining "average" is really simple math:

> Average = apathy
>
> Average = living a "settle for" life
>
> Average = just comfortable
>
> Average = "my four and no more"
>
> Average = passionless living
>
> Average = never creating waves
>
> Average = paralysis of purpose
>
> And, Average + anything = less than God intended!

As you can see, "average" and the King's DNA don't mix!

I've yet to meet a child whose dream was to be average. At one point and time, they all dream of being a super hero. (Actually, that's the concept behind the cover of this book.) Kids dream of being doctors, rock stars, astronauts, firemen, actors/actresses, professional athletes, etc. But as life unfolds, something tragic happens: The enemy called "average" raises its ugly head.

Ninety-five percent of people I meet are living very average lives—some even below. They live in an average house, work at an average job, exist in an average marriage, carry average debt, take average vacations, drive average cars, make average accomplishments, enjoy average amount of happiness, live an average lifespan, and will probably die an average death and be buried in an average coffin! The only thing *above* average is that they're grieved more than an average amount of time because of their average life and how they accomplish far below average results for the Kingdom of God.

This might be your life right now, but it doesn't have to be. Have you ever thought, *How does God think about being average?* Actually, quite a bit.

To begin with, one of His names is El Shaddai, which means, "The God who is more than enough." Contrary to what you may have heard, He's not God of just the "thirty, sixty, or one hundred-fold." He's more than you could ever imagine. That's exactly what Ephesians 3:20 says, that He's:

> ***"…able to do immeasurably more than we can ask or think, according to the power that works within us,"***

> (NIV)

Another example is to look where God lives. There's nothing about Heaven that's average in anyone's estimation. On and on the Bible clearly describes your Heavenly Father as One who lives up to His name: more than enough. There has never been, nor will there ever be anything "average" about Him—and that's exactly how He's designed you to live.

You most definitely have an enemy called "average." It's out to break your focus, sedate you, and destroy God's plans for your life. But it doesn't have to any longer.

It's time to make the change.

MAKE THE CHANGE

If you're not living the life God has destined for you right now, there's one main culprit: the lack of applied information. That's about to change.

Yes, God indeed watches over His Word to perform it, but you have a responsibility, too. It's not God's Word sitting in between the index and the maps in your Bible that will change you; it's His Word engrafted into your heart. That's the Word He can—and will—perform. (See James 1:21.) That's why this book's DNA is straight from the Bible.

 B.B.: Whatever stirs your emotions will lead you to your purpose.

I know you're ready to destroy your enemy and live the way God engineered you—in abundance. This book is strategically designed to help you do just that. Each chapter is a specific step to help break through that barrier and move you to the place of significance.

My purpose is very evident: helping move people out of the slump of mediocrity. It's also no secret that I loathe "average." By the time you're done with this book, you will too! Not only will you detest it, you will also have the tools to defeat it.

So, are you ready to defeat this wicked foe? I know you are. Attack!

CHAPTER 3

DO MORE THAN EXIST...LIVE

COME WITH ME to West Texas during the Great Depression. Mr. Ira Yates was like many other ranchers during that era: He owned a lot of land, and had a lot of debt. With the country in economic turmoil, Mr. Yates's sheep ranching operation wasn't profitable enough to pay his mortgage. Consequently, he was in grave danger of losing his ranch. With little money for clothes or food, his family (like many others) had to rely on a government subsidy.

While watching his sheep graze over the rolling West Texas hills day after day, Mr. Yates was greatly troubled over paying his bills and supporting his family. Little did he know that was all about to change.

One day, an oil company's seismographic crew came into the area. After several days of testing, they approached the struggling sheep rancher with great news: "Mr. Yates, we believe there may be oil underneath your land." When asked permission to drill a wildcat well on his property, Mr. Yates agreed and signed the contract. The rest is history.

Just over a thousand feet below the surface, the drillers struck a huge oil reserve. When production started that first well produced eighty thousand barrels a day! It was just the beginning. Many subsequent wells produced more than twice that amount. In fact, thirty years after the initial discovery, a government test showed one well had the potential to produce one hundred and twenty-five thousand barrels of oil…per day!

 B.B.: We tend to live unaware of our vast fortune.

And Mr. Yates owned it all.

You see, from the very first day he purchased that land, Ira Yates owned all the oil and mineral rights. Yet he was living on government relief. A multimillionaire living in poverty. What was the breakdown? Simple. He had no idea what was rightfully his.

I think it's fair to say that many Christians are a lot like Mr. Yates at times. We are heirs to a rich life—a life filled with adventure and promise—yet we live far below what is rightfully ours. Jesus described that life in John 10:10 when He said:

> *"I have come that they may have life, and that they may have it more abundantly."*

The New International Version of that same verse reads:

> *"I have come that they may have life, <u>and have it to the full</u>."*

Jesus wasn't the only one who described this life. The Apostle Peter said it this way:

"...His divine power has given to us all things that pertain to life and godliness ... "

2 Peter 1:3

Why did God provide this abundant life for all Believers? John 15:11 tells us exactly why:

"These things I have spoken to you, that My joy may remain in you, and that your joy may be _full_."

It's very obvious what God is saying: *"Do more than exist—LIVE."*

THE UPPER

It doesn't take long to realize that God's idea of "living" and the world's definition are quite opposite. The world says, "Make a living." God says, "Build a life." To do so you must be purposeful in your pursuit. "Average" is a very crowded space. You must aim high and live above the norm. When you do you'll soon realize that the air is thinner at higher altitudes, but it's also where the excitement is!

While vacationing in Colorado, my wife Donna and I decided to go white-water rafting down the Animas River. We found an outfitter, and while selecting our gear the guide asked us, "Do you want to raft the lower or upper Animas?" I responded, "What's the difference?" She said, "Most people do the lower section because it's a little gentler." Donna immediately looked at me with her pleading eyes, which prompted me to quickly say, "The upper Animas, please!"

Our guide, who looked like she was barely out of high school, was shocked. "Sir," she said, "you do know the upper section is all Class V rapids and above, don't you? We don't even have any guides to go with you. The few we had were all killed there, and we never found their bodies." (Okay, she didn't really say the last part, but that's pretty much what Donna heard!)

That day, over two hundred rafts floated down the lower Animas River. The upper? Just two: us and one other brave couple. It wound up being one of the most exhilarating days of our lives! Not just being on the river, but the fact that Donna didn't kill me when I said, "The upper." It was such a rush, here I am still talking about it.

Two hundred rafts on the *average* portion of the river; two on the "clean your drawers when you're done" portion. When you think about it, aren't these statistics fairly true in life, too? For every person who's living the all out, thrilling, meaningful life, there are hundreds—maybe even thousands—who aren't. Which one are you? It's time to live the "upper" life. Why?

Because time is running out.

WHAT'S THE MEASURE?

A few years ago, *People Magazine* published an article entitled, "Dead Ahead." It told of a new clock that tracks how much time you have left to live. The clock calculates an average life span of seventy-five years for men and eighty years for women. The calculations were simple. You basically program your sex and age into the clock, and from then on it tells you how much time you have left on this earth.

Oh, and it sold for a mere $99.95.

You probably can guess that I didn't buy one. The reason

was simple: While this clock can measure the amount of years left in my life, *it can't measure the amount of life left in my years!* That's up to me. And the same is true for you.

Time is the currency of life. Five hundred and twenty-five thousand, six hundred minutes in a year. Once they've passed you can never get even one of them back. Multi-billionaire investor mogul, Mark Cuban, once said, "Money you can make or lose. Time, you can only lose." How are you investing your time? Are you simply trading it for a paycheck? If you desire to live a better life, what is your growth plan? What is your health plan? Do you even have a plan?

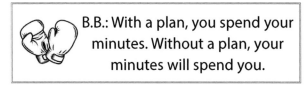

B.B.: With a plan, you spend your minutes. Without a plan, your minutes will spend you.

And that's why countless millions of people only *exist* and don't *live*.

GOD'S DESIRES/YOUR DESIRES

One of the best ways to move from existing to living is to identify what makes you feel most alive and then pursue it. Do you love photography? Then start experimenting with whatever camera you have—even your cell phone camera. Subscribe to a photography magazine. Read photography blogs that allow you to chat with others and display some of your work. Join a photography club. Take some classes at your local community college. The opportunities are endless.

Two things which really make me feel truly alive are

traveling and ministry. Whenever I have the opportunity to combine the two, as the saying goes, "I'm already there!" Those two passions have allowed me to minister all across America and in twenty-one different countries on four different continents.

 B.B.: When you are pursuing a passion, you will be energized with life.

Psalm 37:4 is true. God really does grant us our heart's desires. Not only did He place those desires in us, He also helps us discover what they are. Of course, I've had people say, "Well, Ron, I have a lot of desires that God ain't brought to pass." I'm sure that's right. How do I know? Because I'm in that very same boat. I mean, I'm still waiting for someone to hand me $20,000 and say, "God told me you wanted to go back to the Swiss Alps. So, here ya go!"

Maybe, one day soon.

If you will, allow me to use the following scripture a bit out of context to make a point. (At least I asked.) Hebrews 6:11-12 says:

> *"And we desire that each of you show the same diligence to the full assurance of hope until the end, that you do not become sluggish, but imitate those who through faith and patience inherit the promises."*

I realize the writer of Hebrews is talking about the promises of God here; however, I find great uniformity in the way God operates. Follow me for a moment. If He gives us the desires of our hearts, is it possible that the realization of those desires might, at times, require some faith and patience? I know they have for me.

Without a lot of faith, patience, and diligence, I would have never walked the Holy Land, ministered to thousands of people in Ethiopia, Haiti, India, Central and South America, and many European nations, plus experienced many other wonders of life. Was it expensive? Are you kidding me? NO! Compared to what not experiencing these things would have cost me in the currency of life, it was very inexpensive.

> B.B.: Existing is always costlier than living

Never let your enemy try and convince you otherwise.

NOT JUST FOR YOU

I can attest that there's nothing like really living. It's the best (and really the only) life to live. It's true because when you really live, not only do you reap the benefits, others do as well.

In following my God-given passions and desires, I've seen tumors fall to the floor, blind eyes open, and the lame run! I've brought Kingdom truths, taught leadership skills, and minis-tered hope to countless thousands of people. You might think, *Now, Ron, isn't that just you bragging a bit?* Yes, it is...I'm brag-ging on my God. *He's* the One who put those desires in me. *He* honored my faith and patience. *He* touched and healed people through me. And in those moments that He was working, I've never been so alive!

It's okay to live your passions and brag on your God. Of course, your enemy will always ask, "Who do you think you are?" If you listen and believe this garbage, you'll never pursue what infuses life into you. However, when you pursue a Godly desire and good comes out of it (and it always will when He's the author), the enemy will then tell you, "Shut up and don't brag about it." Make no mistake, no matter what you do your enemy will always find a way to discredit you.

So, you might as well go ahead and live and stop only existing!

TODAY!

I once heard a story of a man who had a checkup with his doctor. When we went back to review the results, the doctor told him, "Well, I have bad news and worse news. Which do you want to hear first?" The man, a bit taken aback, said, "Well, give me the bad news first." The doctor said, "Okay, the bad news is that you only have twenty-four hours to live." This distraught man immediately jumped up and shouted, "Twenty-four hours to live? What could possibly be worse?" The doctor replied, "Well, I was supposed to tell you yesterday but I forgot."

Of course, this is only a joke, but it does make you think: How hard would you pursue what infuses life into you if you didn't have long to live?

Think about it. If the doctor said that you were dying, how different would your life look? What things have you been putting off would suddenly grab your attention? Who would you show great appreciation towards? What places would you see?

What projects would you complete? Now, I'm not your doctor, but may I give you a stark realization?

You are dying!

That's right. Everyone is in the dying process. In fact, the day you drew your very first breath started the journey to your last one. That's one reason why you should live every day like it's your last. One day, it will be.

What's the most valuable real estate in your city? Is it the downtown property? The waterfront lots? The upscale gated development? No, it's none of these. The most valuable pieces of real estate in every city are the graveyards. You read it correctly: the graveyards. In those plots of land lie buried movies, plays, poetry, inventions, medical breakthroughs, books, music, etc. Not to mention the love never shown, the dreams never lived, and the goals never met. All just six-feet under the surface.

What am I saying? Make the most of every day. Live every day to its fullest and go out of this world totally empty. No, "I love you's" unsaid. No forgiveness un-given. No books unwritten. No happiness un-spread. Nothing left undone, unspoken, or unpursued. That's the life to live...but it doesn't just "happen." You must make it a priority.

Do you need to shift some priorities around? If so, don't wait. "Someday" is not one of the days of the week. "Someday" never comes. Do it today.

One day *will* be your last.

THE ROAD OF LIFE

French-German theologian, Albert Schweitzer, once said, "The tragedy of life is what dies inside a person when they live." I can fully relate to this statement. You see, this book has been inside me for fifteen years, and has taken over ten years to write. But I finally did it. And it feels as though what was dead inside of me is now alive.

During the writing process, I found myself regretting the past while fearing the future all at the same time. It was during one of those moments when I heard the Lord speak to my heart: "My name is I Am." He then paused. I waited to hear more. Then He continued, "When you live in the past, with its mistakes and regrets, life is hard. I am not there. My name is not I Was. When you live in the future, with its problems and fears, life is hard. I am not there, either. My name is not I Will Be. But, when you live in this moment, living is not hard. I am there. My name is I Am!"

One word from God completely changed my perception of Him and gave me the motivation to finish what He had put inside me to do.

That's my story. What about you? What tactic is your enemy using to keep the things inside you dormant? Is it the regret of past failures? Fear of the unknown? Self-confidence issues? No matter what is being used against you, it's time for it all to come to a stop, today. You were fashioned by the Creator of the universe. He's the One who gave you those desires. So, come on, come on, *come on*! Discover them...

...And then do them!

When you make this jump, let me assure you that a life lived above average will have more discomforts than your average, ho-hum life. That's the price tag of living instead of existing. Maybe that's why most people walk through life with their foot on the brakes rather than the accelerator. But that's not you.

When things get tough (and they will), remember the words of Jesus:

"These things I have spoken to you, that in Me you may have peace. In the world you will have tribulation; but be of good cheer, I have overcome the world."

John 16:33

 B.B.: Real living is always worth the price.

You are *in* the world, but not *of* the world. Jesus has overcome the world and you are in Him. Tribulations will come, trials will show up, difficulties will be waiting around the corner. Let them come. They will have no harmful effects on you. Why? Because you are in Him. Whatever the world throws at you, Jesus has already defeated it.

The great Apostle Paul knew a thing or two about living... and the trials that accompanied that life. In one passage he described his life this way:

"...I am more: in labors more abundant, in stripes above measure, in prisons more frequently, in deaths often. From the Jews five times I received forty stripes minus one. Three times I was beaten with rods; once I was stoned; three times I was shipwrecked; a night and a day I have been in the deep; in journeys often, in perils of waters, in perils of robbers, in perils of my own countrymen, in perils of the Gentiles, in perils in the city, in perils in the wilderness, in perils in the sea, in perils among false brethren; in weariness

and toil, in sleeplessness often, in hunger and thirst, in fastings often, in cold and nakedness—besides the other things, what comes upon me daily..."

2 Corinthians 11:23-28

Reading this might give you the tendency to put on the brakes and avoid stuff like Paul went through. I've been in positions when I've thought, *Whoa, I never signed up for this!* It would've been easy to revert back to average. But this is what I've learned: When you put the brakes on life due to uncomfortable situations, you also put a halter on all the great things life has to offer. The solution?

 B.B.: Keep your foot on the accelerator pedal, no matter what.

In the words of my long-time friend, Sherman Owens, "All the water in the world can't drown you if you don't let it get in your boat."

Despite all the hardships, Paul lived a life that was anything *but* average. He spoke before kings, traveled most of the known world, healed the sick, raised the dead, and was responsible (directly or indirectly) for mass millions receiving eternal life. Paul didn't just have his name written in the Bible; God used him to write nearly two-thirds of the New Testament. What a life!

Think about it. What if Paul was more interested in merely existing than really living? What if he would've stayed home, watched television and avoided all the pain? What a tragic price to pay. Praise God, Paul didn't succumb to "average." He didn't settle for existing. Paul endured…and lived.

So will you.

GET STARTED NOW

As you can see, there's no real life in only existing. Life is in living! But if all the encouragement in this chapter isn't enough motivation to let off the brakes and step on the gas, then maybe seeing how God looks at an "average' life will do it. Take a look at what He said to the church at Laodicea:

> *"I know your works, that you are neither cold nor hot. I could wish you were cold or hot. So then, because you are lukewarm, and neither cold nor hot, I will vomit you out of My mouth."*

Revelation 3:15-16

Whoa! Did you read that? It pretty obvious that a "lukewarm" life equals just existing. In that light this scripture is saying:

It's time to stop the excuses, throw away the justifications, and start living. You deserve it. Your family deserves it. Everyone connected to you in any way deserves it. So start now. Start with you.

B.B.: If you want to make God puke, then simply exist.

Let me close this chapter with the words from an unknown monk recorded in AD 1100: "When I was a young man, I wanted to change the world. I found it was difficult to change the world, so I tried to change my nation. When I found I couldn't change my nation, I began to focus on my town. I couldn't change the town. As an older man, I tried to change my family. Now, as an old man, I realize the only thing I can change is myself. Suddenly, I realize that if long ago I had changed myself, I could have made an impact on my family. My family and I could have made an impact on our town. Their impact could have changed the nation, and I could indeed have changed the world."

It's time to change your life and start living…really living. When you do you'll give others permission to do the same. It's time to face the obstacles that come with living an exceptional life and overcome them. Do you want to break through the barrier called average? Then stop existing…

…Start living!

CHAPTER 4

DO MORE THAN LISTEN...HEAR

STEVE MORRIS WAS a not-so-popular third-grader who lived in Michigan. He was, as some would say, "different." Not only was he different, he was extremely smart. So, Steve had two strikes against him that caused avoidance by the other kids: he was blind, making him "different," and he always had the right answers when called on by his teacher, Mrs. Beneducci. Steve's schooling was a lonely existence. That was before the day everything changed.

As Mrs. Beneducci started to write on the chalkboard that day, she heard a light scratching noise. She said, "Quiet, class. What's that noise?" Everyone listened for a few seconds, and then one of the kids yelled, "It's a mouse!" Pandemonium broke out in the classroom. The girls quickly jumped to the top of their desks, screaming at the top of their lungs, while all the boys scurried to find the culprit. All the boys—except for Steve Morris.

Mrs. Beneducci quieted the class and regained ordered. However, the scratching noise could still be heard on occasion. She finally told the class, "I sure wish I could find the mouse." Steve Morris replied, "I know where it is." Whether Steve was telling the truth or simply looking for class acceptance, no one will ever know. What we do know is that he was right, and change was about to happen.

The third-grade teacher responded, "Well, Mr. Morris, if you know where it is, please show us." Steve rose from his desk, walked to the front of the class, and stopped at the trash can just to the left of his teacher's desk. Then he said, "It's in there." Sure enough, after removing some papers, there sat the mouse. It was safely captured and became the class mascot.

While everyone else in the room was captivated by the mouse, Mrs. Beneducci's attention was drawn to another phenomenon—Steve. How could he know where that mouse was hiding? Everyone else heard the same noise, but only Steve could precisely pinpoint its location. Of this amazing ability to hear, Mrs. Benducci said, "Steve, you're a wonder." She was right. Today, he's still known by that name. That's the day Steve Morris became Stevie Wonder, the world-renown recording artist.

What made Steve such a "wonder"? His ability to hear. He's not alone. The same can be true for you. Your ability to hear what others don't—or won't—can be a game changer as well.

WHO GETS THE PRIZE?

Many years ago, the telegraph was the fastest method of long-distance communication. During this time, a young man answered an ad in the local newspaper for a job as a Morse Code operator. When he arrived at the address listed, he entered a large, busy office filled with noise and clatter—including the sound of a telegraph in the background. He knew he was in the right place.

A sign on the receptionist's counter instructed job applicants to fill out a form and then wait until summoned to enter the office. This young man filled out his form and then waited his turn with the seven other applicants already in the waiting area.

After a few minutes, the young man stood up, crossed the room in front of the other applicants, and entered into the inner office. Naturally, the other seven were wondering what exactly was happening. They muttered amongst themselves as to why they hadn't been summoned? Their comfort was assuming this young man made a mistake and would be disqualified from the candidacy.

They were wrong.

Within a few minutes, the employer escorted this young man out of the inner office and said to the other applicants, "Gentlemen, thank you for coming, but the job has just been filled." As grumblings broke out, one applicant spoke up. "Wait a minute. I don't understand. He was the last one to come in. We never got a chance to even interview. That's not fair!" The employer calmly responded, "I'm sorry, but for the last several minutes, while all of you have been sitting here, the telegraph has been sending out this message in Morse Code: 'If you can hear this message, come right in. The job is yours.' Only one of you responded. So the job is his." The same is true in life.

 B.B.: The prize goes to the hearer.

A LOST ART

Talkers are a dime a dozen. Just think about the relationships you enjoy the most. Think about the people you allow the greatest access to your life. How about the ones you know truly value your heart? What do they all have in common? They really *hear* you.

A young man once approached Socrates, asking to be taught the gift of oratory. His request was followed by an incessant stream of words. Finally, Socrates placed his hand over the inquirer's mouth and said, "Young man, I will have to charge you a double fee." The lad asked, "Why?" Socrates replied, "I will have to teach you two sciences. First, how to hold your tongue, and then, how to use it."

It's sad, but hearing is a lost art. For years, we've heard the adage: "The reason God gave you two ears and one mouth is so you can hear twice as much as you speak." I think it has somehow lost its meaning.

Do you want to have some fun exploiting the fact that many people don't really hear? Here's one way. Tell someone the following: "You are driving a bus. At the first stop, eight people get on the bus. At the next stop, ten people get off, but six get on. Now, how old is the driver?" Most will contemplate the figures, but the answer is simple: You began with "YOU are driving a bus." They're the bus driver!

In telling this you'll find that most don't hear. Thus, it paints a great point. Even though they might have listened to your question, they failed to hear what you really said.

Over the years I've been able to do much marriage counseling. It's a blessing when couples later say things like, "Ron, you're a genius. You saved our marriage." Or, "Because of you, we're in love again." It all sounds good, but don't believe them. It's a bunch of hooey! I'm surely not a genius, nor did I "save" their marriage. What made things turn around came down to one basic element: they began to really hear each other again.

They found the lost art.

I've also mediated situations where if arbitration failed, the two parties were headed to court. It's interesting to see how each side is so focused on their side of the story, they don't hear what the other is saying. In my experience—just like with marriages—if the two parties can reach a point where they truly hear one another, things invariably turn around. Unfortunately, only one non-hearer can cause the whole matter to continue down a very tough road.

Oh, how I wish someone would have taught me earlier the great and vast value of holding my tongue and using my ears. Almost every tough situation I've created in my life can be linked to one problem: I didn't take time to hear. That's one reason I firmly believe hearing is the greatest people skill on the face of the earth.

It's time to regain its value.

HE HEARS, SO CAN YOU

I'm sure you've never experienced the frustration of giving instructions to a child, an employee, a volunteer, or your spouse only to have them completely ignore it. Oh, wait. You have? Welcome to life! I have too. It's one of those things that makes me want to lay hands on them...suddenly. Of course, I'm sure God has desired to do the same to His kids every now and then.

Speaking of God.

He is the best hearer in the universe.

In my thirty years of walking with the Lord, one of His many attributes still amazes me: He hears us. You might be thinking, *How could that be sooooo amazing?* I'm glad you asked. Track with me for a minute.

Light travels at eighty-six thousand miles per second. That's seven times around the earth in one second. One second! Travelling at that speed, it would take you one hundred thousand *years* to cross our little Milky Way Galaxy, not to mention the eight-hundred billion other galaxies out there. What's my point? The One who holds this kind of expanse in the palm of His hand…takes time to *hear you.*

That's exactly what the Bible says, too. One of my favorite scriptures is 1 John 5:14-15:

> ***"Now this is the confidence that we have in Him, that if we ask anything according to His will, He hears us. And if we know that He hears us, whatever we ask, we know that we have the petitions that we have asked of Him."***

Since it's true that God hears you, and if you are to be perfect like Him, then you have the ability to be a hearer, too. Notice I said, "a hearer," not just a listener.

We all have a lot to listen to, but very little of what we hear is allowed to enter into the level classified as "truly hearing." Even Jesus said in Mark 4:24, "Pay attention to what you hear." Pay attention to what? What you hear. If it's possible *to* pay attention, then it's reasonable to deduce that you have the ability to *not* pay attention, right? That's called casual listening, and it's way different than intentional hearing.

In Matthew 13:13 Jesus also said, "I speak to them in parables, because seeing they do not see, and hearing they do not hear." This "hearing without hearing" is a big deal to Jesus. Chances are, you're listening to much, but are you really hearing what's important? Listening is easy; really hearing requires much more discipline.

Here are few other scriptures which all address the power of this subject:

> *"So then, my beloved brethren, let every man be swift to hear, slow to speak..."*

James 1:19

> *"<u>Listen</u> to counsel and receive instruction, that you may be wise in your latter days."*

Proverbs 19:20

> *"In the multitude of words sin is not lacking, but he who restrains his lips is wise."*

Proverbs 10:19

You will also find the phrase, "He who has ears to hear, let him hear," three times in the book of Matthew and eight times in the book Revelation. I don't know about you, but I think God is trying to get a point across.

Hearing is better than listening.

PUT IT TO WORK

Okay, enough talk on hearing. Time to put it to work. And here are some great ways to start:

- Ask three people who know you fairly well if they think you have a great ability to hear the heart of those communicating with you. Oh, and make sure one of the three is someone you're *not* getting along with very well at the moment. Yes, it may not be fair, but it makes my point. If you're not in good relationship right now, it probably means someone isn't hearing someone else very well.

  That someone may be you.

- The next time you're engaged in a meaningful (which can sometimes be loud) conversation with someone, say this, "I think what I'm hearing you say is…" and then repeat what you heard. After they pick themselves off the floor, you can resume your normal conversation!

  Don't be artificial. State that phrase back in whatever way is natural for you. Make sure you're conveying that there could be room for error between what was said and what you heard. And leave all the negative emotion (aka drama) at the front door. The goal is not to scrutinize but to really, truly learn to hear.

Saint Augustine said: "What does love look like? It has the hands to help others. It has the feet to hasten to the poor and needy. It has eyes to see misery and want. It has the ears to hear the sighs and sorrows of men. That is what love looks like." How true it is. Not only does hearing take courage, it also accomplishes another feat: *it destroys the enemy called average!*

You know you're on your way to life way above "average" when you learn to stop listening...

　　...And start really hearing.

CHAPTER 5

DO MORE THAN AGREE...
COOPERATE

WHILE THERE HAS been much teaching on the power of agreement (and thank God for it), there is another step obtained by those who refuse to live an average life. It's called cooperation. Let's start by seeing what that word means.

The prefix *co-* means, "together." The remainder of the word, *operate*, means, "working successfully." When joined together, to cooperate simply means "Together, working successfully." That's drastically different than just agreeing with someone. You can agree with someone on a matter yet not lift a finger to help accomplish it. Cooperation takes the next step—laying all pettiness aside to work successfully with one another.

To live your fullest life, you must learn the art of cooperation on two different levels: one with God, and one with people. Let's examine both in further detail.

COOPERATION WITH GOD

Cooperating with God starts by aligning yourself to His will for your life. Think of it this way: Suppose you were stranded in the middle of a lake and threw a hook on a rope to the shore. When you tug on the rope, are you pulling the shore to you, or you to the shore? Of course, you're pulling yourself to the shore. It's the same with cooperating with God. It's not pulling God to your will, but bringing yourself into what He has ordained for your life.

You've probably heard this a million times, but it's true: God has a divine plan for your life. And, contrary to what you may have heard before, it's a *great* plan. One that is custom fit to your personality, desires, likes, interest, passions, etc. I mean, God placed all these things in you to begin with, so why would he create a life-plan that doesn't actuate them? That's not the God you serve. He's your good Heavenly Father with a marvelous plan for you, His kid.

The quicker you cooperate with Him and His will, the less you will struggle in life. Quit trying to have everything your way and then wonder, *Where is God?* when things go wrong. Throw out your hook to the shore (it's not as far as you think) and give it a tug. He's ready to have you a bit closer.

"I'M LEAVING!"

I'll never forget the most confounding words God ever spoke to me. Standing in front of a tent in Ethiopia, God said, "Ron, I'm leaving you!" Not only was I taken back by His words, but considering the task that lay in front of me, they couldn't have come at a worse time. (I know Hebrews 13:5 says, "I'll never leave you or forsake you," but He was making a point with me.)

A team of us were finishing up a multi-day evangelistic crusade. Each day, we saw hundreds of thousands of people in attendance. On the last day, we set up a tent behind the platform for those who were too sick to be in the audience but desired prayer. After the meeting, four of us journeyed back to the tent to pray for people. What awaited us was more than shocking... it was practically unbelievable.

When we pulled back the flap, I couldn't believe my eyes. The tent was full of people with open wounds, growths, tumors—things I'd never even imagined. Misery and moaning filled the air, along with a stench that was indescribable. No one had any idea what diseases were oozing all over these semi corpses, and I wasn't very motivated to find out.

The other three guys just jumped in! I'd love to say that I put on my Holy Ghost flamethrower, lifted my shield of faith, and charged that hellish nightmare...but I didn't. Far from it. I was scared half to death. I thought, *There's no way I'm going in there!* (I might even have said it out loud. I was too scared to remember.) It was at that moment that God said, "Ron, you can stay out here if you want, but I'm going in there. I'm leaving you." Now, I'm not the sharpest knife in the drawer, but right then it dawned on me that I'd probably be better off in a disease-infested tent *with* God than outside *without* Him!

So, in I went.

I laid my hands on stuff you couldn't even imagine that day. But, He was with me. Why? Because I made the decision to align myself with Him, even though it wasn't pretty. Now, years later, I can tell this story without any shame. I'm a better person, and many Ethiopians are better because I cooperated with God and pulled myself to His shore.

YOUR MOVE

Sailing late into a foggy night, a ship's captain could faintly see some lights in the distance. He immediately told his signalman to send the message, "Alter your course ten degrees south." A prompt message came back in return, "Alter your course ten degrees north." Angered that his command had been ignored, the captain sent a second message, "Alter your course ten degrees south. I am a captain." Again, a quick response, "Alter your course ten degrees north. I am third-class seaman Jones." Now furious, the captain messaged, "Alter your course ten degrees south. I am a battleship." And then the reply that settled the standoff: "Alter your course ten degrees north. I am a lighthouse!"

Isn't that what we do when trying to negotiate with God? We want to tell God how to alter His plan for our lives, when in turn He says, "I am the Creator of the universe. You make the adjustment!"

So, the question is how can you know the will of God for your life? The primary way is to know His Word. God's Word is God's will. It's the "Winner's Digest." The manual for "How to live on planet earth and like it." The Word of God very concisely and clearly instructs us regarding His will. It's the lighthouse, so to speak. I don't care how big and bad you may think you are or how much you might have it all together, I have news for you: His ways are higher than yours!

Whatever you have to do, pull yourself to God with all your might. Cooperate—work successfully together—with Him. It's the best life you can possibly imagine.

It's the life far above "average."

COOPERATION WITH OTHERS

When I was younger, my two brothers and I were very cooperative. We cooperated in a grand scheme to do each other in! One such incident comes to the front of my mind.

Our parents had not been on a date since we were all born. For the first time in about fifteen years (I was twelve or thirteen years old at the time.), they decided the time had come where us boys could be left at home alone, and they could enjoy an evening together. It didn't take long for mischief to set in and do its damage.

When they left, I set out on a motorcycle ride across our family farm. During my ride, I spotted my older brother walking across the yard. I did what any "normal" twelve-year-old would do: I headed straight for him. Let me say that what transpired after my decision was completely his fault! If he would have only kept walking, everything would have been fine. But when he saw me making a bee-line for him, he froze.

Of course, I didn't allow enough margin of error for that. I swerved as hard as I could, only clipping the back of his heel. What happened next seems almost physically impossible. How I wish we had a video camera back in those days. We would have won the World's Funniest Video's $100,000 grand prize!

My brother was not hurt in the least. Me, well that's a different story altogether.

What started as an innocent motorcycle ride turned into a Chuck Yeager test flight. I remember flying through the air for what seemed like a half mile (it was probably only about twenty feet.). When I landed, my head caught the corner of a four by four post lying on the ground. I was unaware of any injury, but I knew something was amiss once my brother stopped laughing, turned white as a ghost, and pointed his finger at me. And for good reason. Looking down at my shoulder I saw a river of blood flowing from my head.

My parents had just settled into their movie—popcorn in hand—when the page came. A short stay at the hospital, along with some morphine and stitches, and I was good as new.

This was just one in a long list of incidents between us boys. Being about three years apart from each other, we couldn't get along for anything. We would punch, poke, prod, and provoke each other until some nuclear holocaust broke out among us. Though the word "orphanage" was thrown around quite a bit, my parents never followed through on that threat, for which I am eternally grateful.

But another threat came along.

One year, we found ourselves students in a new school. Not just any ol' school, mind you. This was our old school's rival. From the first day, there were a lot of kids who didn't like us. But that turned out to be a good thing. Literally within one day, my two brothers and I turned our attention and commitment towards each other. We were "thick as thieves." We had a motto: If you messed with one of us, you messed with all of us.

What happened? We had a rallying point. No longer did it matter if we walked in agreement or disagreement; now we were walking in cooperation. And, it felt good. Really good. That season of deep stupidity taught me a powerful lesson:

 B.B.: Cooperation is the essence of Godliness.

The Bible also concludes this fact.

FIND THE ROPES

The world as it was known completely changed fifty days after the resurrection of Jesus. It's the day we call Pentecost Sunday. Not only was God a major factor behind the happenings of that day, the people on earth—cooperating with God and each other—played a huge role as well. Acts 2:1 explains how:

> *"When the Day of Pentecost had fully come, they were all with one accord in one place."*

And the planet hasn't been the same since!

The Greek word translated into the phrase, "with one accord," is *homothumadon.* It's a very expressive word which signifies how everyone's mind, affections, desires, and wishes were concentrated on one object. All one-hundred and twenty had the same earnest desire and the same end in sight. They all prayed one prayer to God. No one was disinterested or unconcerned. They cooperated with God and with each other. The results? God met their united faith and prayer by pouring out His Spirit on the earth in full measure!

The same is true today. When God's people meet in that same spirit of unity, they can expect to receive every blessing they need. That's the power of working together successfully.

David described a beautiful picture of this in Psalm 133:1-3. He wrote:

> *"Behold, how good and how pleasant it is for brethren to dwell together in unity (cooperating with one another). It is like the precious oil upon the head, running down on the beard, the beard of Aaron,*

running down on the edge of his garments. It is like the dew of Hermon, descending upon the mountains of Zion; For there the LORD commanded the blessing—life forevermore."

There are so many great truths to unpack from these scriptures, but I want you to notice a particular phrase in the last verse: "For there the Lord commands the blessing." Where does God command the blessing? There. Where is there? *Any place where people are cooperating with each other!*

William Carey, the father of modern missions, was a great example of this principle in action. He once told his churches, "If you will hold the ropes, I will go down to look for the lost." Starting with only six supporters, he went to India…and wound up staying forty-seven years. William Cary's evangelic efforts set the entire modern missionary movement in motion.

All with six faithful partners.

The lesson from this story is simple: Find someone's ropes to hold on to! If you will, you will reap someone holding your ropes. To live in God's commanded blessings, simply agreeing won't cut it. You have to be in cooperation with one with another.

There's no place better on earth.

GET TO THAT PLACE

When a six foot four inch, muscularly built Middle Eastern man tried to light an explosive hidden in his shoe on a flight from Paris to Miami, he was tackled by a flight attendant and five passengers. Because six people—who didn't even know each other—cooperated together, a terrible tragedy was averted and all one hundred and ninety-seven people on board that flight were saved!

You see, there's power in cooperation.

Jesus Himself modeled this type of sacrificial cooperation for a greater good. Philippians 2:7-8 says:

> *"but (Jesus) made Himself of no reputation, taking the form of a bondservant, and coming in the likeness of men. And being found in appearance as a man, He humbled Himself and became obedient to the point of death, even the death of the cross."*

Paul actually starts this passage by saying, "Let this mind be in you which was also in Christ Jesus," (Philippians 2:5). In fact, the entire first part of Philippians Chapter 2 admonishes us to cooperate with one another in two ways: (1.) esteeming others more than ourselves, and (2.) looking after others' interests along with our own.

B.B.: Cooperation isn't always easy or fun, but it's always beneficial.

How do you know when you're cooperating with others? One way to know is when these five phrases become part of your vocabulary:

- The five most important words are: "You did a good job."

- The four most important words are: "What is your opinion?"

- The three most important words are: "Let's work together."
- The two most important words are: "Thank you."
- And the single most important word is: "We."

Make it a point to not only cooperate with God but also with others. Remember to work successfully together. It's the only place where we know God *commands* His blessing. And friend, that's the place you want to be!

Agreeing is average. Cooperation brings blessings and life. Do you want to break the barrier of average? Then do more than agree…

…Cooperate.

CHAPTER 6

DO MORE THAN TALK...
COMMUNICATE

WE'VE ALL HEARD the phrase, "Talk is cheap." That may be painfully true, but it shouldn't be.

Take a look around and you'll find that words are everywhere. They're used in phones, iPads, computers, texts, emails, talking navigation systems, Facebook, Twitter, Bluetooth, iPods, etc. Not long ago, I used to talk on the phone for mere minutes a week. Now, on just my cell phone, I talk for hundreds of minutes a week. I used to write a letter maybe two times a year. Now, I write about twenty emails, forty texts, and several social media posts *a day*. It's true, words are everywhere. But, here's the question:

Are we really communicating?

That question reminds me of the couple who shared their thoughts on marriage counseling. The woman said, "Oh, my husband and I never need marriage counseling. We have a great relationship. He was a communications major in college, and I majored in drama. So, he communicates really well and I just act like I'm listening!"

My life—just like yours—is consumed with words. But what are they communicating? I'm afraid for many of us, society has severely diluted what we say. It's to the point that even when our communication is packaged with some deep meaning, it gets lost in the endless sea of words. Maybe we need less talking and more communication.

 B.B.: Just as you can hear without listening, you can talk without communicating.

A DIFFERENT APPROACH

Donna and I went through a time in our marriage where "I love you" was just a routine statement—a tag on the end of every sentence. I would ask, "Donna, what's for dinner?" and she would reply, "I love you." (That usually meant I wasn't getting dinner.) To help us regain the appreciation for this phrase, I decided to repackage it.

One morning, I jumped online and saw what time the sun was setting that evening. I then bought a bottle of sparkling grape juice and snuck it, along with two long-stemmed glasses, into the trunk of the car. That evening I said "Hey, Donna. Let's go for a drive." We only live a few minutes from Siesta Key Beach, one of the top-ten rated beaches in the world, so it was the perfect setting.

When we arrived at the beach, Donna was a bit surprised when I pulled the cooler from the trunk. She asked, "What's in there, Ron?" but I didn't tell her. Then, I spread out a blanket on the white sand. Now, her curiosity was piqued for sure. Just as the sun was setting, I took out the bottle of grape juice and popped the cork. After pouring both of us a glass, I took my beautiful bride by the hand, looked her in the eyes, and said, "I wanted to come to one of the most beautiful spots in the world, to view one of the most beautiful sunsets in the world, and look into the eyes of the most beautiful woman in the world and tell her one thing...'I love you!'"

That one paid dividends for years!

Do you think Donna heard me? Of course she did. Was it more impacting than me just texting her, "I love you."? Of course it was. The key? It was more than just talk. It was communication. And it took our, "I love you" from *average* to *awesome*.

THE WALK

I talk with God every day in prayer. But sometimes, there are some things I really need to communicate to Him. And, at times, there are some things He really needs to communicate to me.

During a particularly saggy droop in my talking with God, I stumbled onto something that has not only changed my communication with Him, it ultimately changed my life. While reading about Enoch walking with God, I began to wonder, *How did he learn to do that?* Then, an amazing revelation started me thinking about a possibility.

I began thinking about how Adam walked with God in the Garden. How special was that? Even though Enoch was seven generations removed from Adam, Adam was still alive at this time. Could it be that Enoch sat on Adam's lap, hearing first-hand accounts of his amazing walks with God in the Garden? I think so. Meditating on this further prompted something in my heart. It wasn't long before I started my own "Enoch walks."

Those times alone with God have been some of the holiest, intimate times in my entire Christian life. So much so, I almost didn't even write about them. But I wanted you to experience what they are all about.

My Enoch walks usually go this way: I start by reading my Bible, then I might listen to a Bible teaching. Next, I pour myself some "revival in a cup" (aka coffee) and head out the door. I've been doing this for about two years now, and I can testify that God *never* fails to show up!

Now, please don't take what I'm about to say out of context, but I've had more intimate times with God on these walks than in my twenty-eight years in church. (Of course, I'm not advocating a substitution for church attendance, but it's the truth.) Why is this? It's because I've positioned myself for more than a talk with God; I'm communicating with Him and Him with me. It's literally changed my entire life.

It just might change yours, too.

MORE THAN ONE WAY

If you don't think things can get lost in translation, then consider the following conversation between a woman and her attorney as a great example:

"I want a divorce."

"Do you have any grounds?"

"Yes, about two acres."

"Do you have a grudge?"

"No, we have a carport."

"Is there infidelity in your marriage?"

"Oh yes. We have a son and a daughter and they both have stereo systems."

"Does your husband beat you up?"

"No, I get up before him every day."

"So then, tell me, what seems to be the problem."

"Oh that's easy, we just can't communicate!"

Just as you can talk and not communicate, you can also communicate without ever speaking one word. Retired U.S. Naval Captain, Gerald Coffee, knew how to employ this principle.

Captain Coffee joined the Navy in 1957 after graduating from UCLA with a degree in commercial art. In 1962, during the Cuban Missile Crisis, Captain Coffee was a crusader pilot who flew F-8 jets on low reconnaissance missions over Cuba. His photos ultimately proved the existence of Soviet missiles there.

In February 1966, while flying combat missions over North Vietnam, his RA5-C reconnaissance jet was shot down by enemy fire. The extremely trained pilot parachuted safely but was immediately captured. For the next seven years and nine days, Captain Coffee was a held as P.O.W. in the communist prisons of North Vietnam. This is where it began.

Where he developed the tap code.

Captain Coffee recalls how he and other P.O.W.s, who were not allowed to speak to each other, communicated without even seeing one another. "By tapping a covert alphabet code on our cell walls, we maintained our unity. We encouraged and cared for each other, passed information, learned poetry, even learned new languages. I got to know my fellow prisoners like brothers, though I'd never even seen them."

Now, you and I will probably never use the tap code, but there are many other non-verbal ways to communicate. One way is through your conduct.

The way you live your life communicates more than you can ever imagine. St. Francis of Assisi has been accredited as once saying, "Preach the gospel every day, and if necessary, use words." That's such great wisdom still today.

 B.B.: You can teach what you want, but you produce what you are.

Consider these passages from Scripture along these lines:

"Who is wise and understanding among you? Let him show by good conduct that his works are done in the meekness of wisdom."

James 3:13

"...but be an example to the believers in word, in conduct, in love, in spirit, in faith, in purity."

1 Timothy 4:12

"Let your light so shine before men, that they may see your good works and glorify your Father in heaven."

Matthew 5:16

B.B: Your mindset comes from other people, but your mind-expanse comes from God.

What are you saying without any words? You've probably heard the saying, "What you are speaks so loud I can't hear what you say." What you communicate without words speaks volumes, but make no mistake, what you say with your words does as well.

Jesus said that by your words are you justified or condemned. (See Matthew 12:37.) Proverbs 16:24 compares pleasant words to honeycomb—sweetness to the soul and health to the bones. It's easy to see that both what you say and the things you don't say each speak of who you are.

RISE ABOVE

People who live average lives only talk. We call average communication "small talk." However, those who rise above the "average" barrier learn and employ the power of real communication. You break the barrier of "average" when you start communicating something—with or without words—to others so that both giver and receiver are blessed.

So, do you want to obliterate "average" and go places in life that you've always dreamed? Then learn to do more than talk...

...Communicate.

CHAPTER 7

DO MORE THAN THINK...RENEW

BEFORE YOU START thinking that I'm telling you not to think, think again! Average people only think; those who live on a higher plane not only think, they also renew their minds to a higher way of thinking.

One of my favorite scriptures is Romans 12:2. It says:

> *"And do not be conformed to this world, but be transformed by the renewing of your mind, that you may prove what is that good and acceptable and perfect will of God."*

A few words in this scripture really stand out.

First, the word "conformed." The prefix *con-* means "artificial; to swindle, trick or commit fraud." The remainder of that word, "formed," means "shaped, modeled, or fashioned." Placed together, we see that being conformed means "to be artificially shaped." This is very significant in understanding the meaning of this scripture. Now read it, "Don't be artificially shaped to the world…" It sounds easy, right? It is, but only by following Paul's next instruction: to be transformed by the renewing of your mind.

The prefix *trans-* means "to change, to cross over, metamorphose." You're surely familiar with the process of metamorphosis. It's when a caterpillar turns into a butterfly. According to the Scripture, that's exactly what happens when you begin renewing your mind. You were a caterpillar; now you're a butterfly. The old you—with the old way of thinking—is dead. "Average" is no longer part of your makeup or thought life. Welcome to the new you:

The you that's alive, thriving, kicking average in the pants, and living abundantly.

THE WAY TO VICTORY

Wouldn't it be great if the movie *Transformers* happened in real life? I mean, how cool would it be if you were instantly transformed into this brand new, larger-than-life person, who only lived in your new reality? It's possible in Hollywood. In life, not so much. Why? Because your enemy would love to keep you "conformed" to your old, average ways.

Everyone loves to see the beautiful butterfly, but what happened to the caterpillar? It's simple. He died. No longer does the butterfly have to deal with what he used to be. It simply doesn't exist any longer. That's exactly what happens to you when you "transform." The old you dies, but your enemy wants to put it on life support.

The Bible describes your adversary as "a roaring lion seeking whom he may devour." (See 1 Peter 5:8.) His job is to try and convince you that the old you isn't dead. He holds up an artificial copy of your old nature—a constant reminder of who you *used* to be and how you *used* to think and act. But here's the truth: It's a fake! A forgery. According to Colossians 3:3, the new you is held in the most secure vault in the universe...with God Himself.

> *"For you died, and your life is hidden with Christ in God."*

The next time your enemy shows up with mental snap shots of the old, average, "caterpillar" you, slithering on the ground and eating leaves, tell him "No, that one's dead!"

My experience has told me that it's pretty difficult for the dead me to sin! In the same manner, your new life in Christ has no propensity to sin. It's much like a bald man using hair spray; there's no place for it. For you to revert back to your old ways would require believing a lie—one that's designed to artificially shape you back into your old world. Don't fall for it. Resist and he will flee.

How can you prove to the enemy that you have a renewed mind? By doing what 2 Corinthians 10:5-6 says to do:

> *"Casting down arguments and every high thing that exalts itself against the knowledge of God, bringing every thought into captivity to the obedience of Christ, and being ready to punish all disobedience when your obedience is fulfilled."*

Two steps: cast down thoughts, punish disobedience with obedience.

When your enemy says something stupid like, "You're not worthy to be talking to God. Besides, you're not disciplined enough anyway," put these scriptures into action. Get up a half hour earlier the next day just to have even more time with your Daddy God. That's casting down and punishing with obedience.

Listen friend, trying to embrace God's promises for your life without being transformed will always be a struggle. So go ahead and cross over. Renew your thought process. Change your outlook. Start to think differently. Once you do, you'll no longer struggle to possess a promise; you will be *possessed by His promises.*

THE NEW YOU

God's thoughts are so much higher than yours, the only way to comprehend them is by a transformed, renewed mind. In 1 Corinthians Chapter 2, Paul tells us that the natural man cannot know the things of the Spirit. That's easy to see. But, he doesn't leave it there. The next verse is far more important to understand:

"...But we have the mind of Christ."

1 Corinthians 2:16

Wow! Did you see what the Bible says about you? That you have the ability to think just like Jesus. And Jesus was anything but "average." What exactly does that look like? I'm glad you asked.

As stated in Chapter 5, Paul says to let your mind be that of Christ Jesus. Then, he continues to explain how Jesus became obedient and died on the cross. Because of His obedience, God exalted Him and made His name greater than any other. So, according to the Bible, the way to have the mind of Christ is simple: Be obedient, die to your old ways, and then watch God and make you great in Him and fulfill His will through you.

Let's break this down. Exactly how do you renew and transform?

- Pray
- Continue major downloads into your mind from the Bible
- Obey
- Die to your old ways
- Meditate

The last step has been stolen from Christianity. When I say, "meditate," I'm not talking about sitting in a yoga position, with your hands in your lap and your middle fingers touching your thumbs, trying to empty your mind. No, when you meditate according to the Bible, you're filling your mind with God's Word.

Joshua 1:8 explains it best:

> *"This Book of the Law shall not depart from your mouth, but you shall meditate in it day and night, that you may observe to do according to all that is written in it. For then you will make your way prosperous, and then you will have good success."*

It's easy to see that dying to your old ways and coming alive to your new life is one sure way to kill the enemy of "average." This is how the Message Bible describes it:

> *"Could it be any clearer? Our old way of life was nailed to the cross with Christ, a decisive end to*

that sin-miserable life—no longer at sin's every beck and call! What we believe is this: If we get included in Christ's sin-conquering death, we also get included in his life-saving resurrection. We know that when Jesus was raised from the dead it was a signal of the end of death-as-the-end. Never again will death have the last word. When Jesus died, he took sin down with him, but alive he brings God down to us. From now on, think of it this way: Sin speaks a dead language that means nothing to you; God speaks your mother tongue, and you hang on every word. You are dead to sin and alive to God. That's what Jesus did."

Romans 6:6-11

BREAK THE BARRIER

I want to end this chapter with a fun and revealing exercise.

Think of a number between one and nine. Multiply that number by nine. Add the digits of your number together (i.e., if 35, then 3 + 5 = 8). Subtract five. Now, if A=1, B=2, C=3 etc., what letter is represented by your number? Do you have it? Good, let's continue.

Think of a country that begins with that letter. Now, think of a mammal that begins with the *last* letter of the country. In the same way, think of a fruit that begins with the *last* letter of the mammal. Got it? You should have a country, an animal, and a fruit. Now, let me see if I can reveal your answer:

Denmark, kangaroo, and an orange.

Surprised? Why didn't you pick a koala, in Denmark, who

likes apples? Or why didn't you pick the Dominican Republic or Djibouti? The truth is, most adults are patterned in their thinking. Children, on the other hand, usually have different alternatives. What exactly is this pattern? It's called containment and conformity. And it's designed, by your enemy, to keep you stuck in the place called "average".

B.B.: Without a renewed mind, you'll be conformed to thinking in the patterns of this world.

It's time to break the mold and *renew* your thinking!

Renewing your mind is quite simple, yet can be a difficult process. It doesn't happen overnight. It takes some time, but *oh, is it worth it.*

It's time to break the barrier. Time to renew your mind by downloading God's thoughts into your thought patterns. When you do, you can kiss your "average" life goodbye! So, do you want to kick "average" in the teeth? Do more than think...

...Renew your mind.

CHAPTER 8

DO MORE THAN GROW...BLOOM

GROWING IS GOOD; blooming is better. Growing is average; blooming is living. Weeds grow, but flowers and trees bloom. When an apple tree blooms, what does it produce? Apples! That's exactly why if you want to destroy the enemy called "average," you must bloom. No, not so that you can eat apples, but so you can produce fruit. In life, you are known by the fruit you produce.

The question is, "Are you positioned to bloom?"

Ecclesiastes 3:10 says that God makes everything beautiful in its time. I'm a walking example of that scripture in action. I didn't used to be beautiful. I am now. Just ask God, my children, my wife, and the people whose lives I've been able to impact. Oh, I can hear you now, "How conceited can one be?" Believe me, it's not conceit...because it's not me.

It's *all* God!

THE MAKING OF RON

Let me explain my statement, "I didn't used to be beautiful." In my B.C. life (Before Christ), I was a mess. I was a young, hard core rock-n-roller who was way beyond an identity crisis. And I looked the part, too: hair down past my shoulder blades and a goatee to boot. I would drink anything, smoke anything, pop anything, and do anything…at least once. What looked like the "party-life" on the outside was nothing short of a growing abyss on the inside.

My life was already spinning out of control when a failed relationship spiraled me into a depth of darkness I never knew existed. Thank God, He spared me through that time, and I started my journey out of darkness. God's grace was renewing me daily, but the whole process was quite comical.

Instead of allowing God to change me (which is always the best way), I decided to take my transformation process into my own hands. The first step was moving from "rocker" to the disco scene. That long hair beyond my shoulder blades turned into a giant afro! At this time, I was six-foot three inches tall and weighed one hundred and sixty pounds, soaking wet. I looked like a broom stick with a huge ball of cotton candy on top! That didn't stop me. I bought some shirts with silver strings and hit the clubs.

Thank goodness, that phase didn't last long. It just wasn't me. So, the next step was "urban cowboy." Yep, I bought a pickup truck, cowboy hat, boots, straight legged jeans, the biggest belt buckle you've ever seen, and hit the bars—even the most famous at the time, Gilley's.

Gilley's, named after the famous country musician, Mickey Gilley, was located in Houston, Texas. What made it stand out above the rest was the mechanical bull. Since I never do anything halfway, I knew I had to ride it at least once. So, I got in line.

A genuine bronc buster-looking guy stood in front of me, so we struck up a conversation. When he found out this was my first time riding, he volunteered some great pointers: "Hold on with your dominant hand, squeeze with your thighs, not your feet, relax your upper body, lean back more than hunkering down, raise your left hand over your head, and point to the top of your head for balance."

Right!

Time for my ride. I climbed up, positioned myself just as my new friend instructed, and nodded at the bull operator. All my she-nanigans didn't impress anyone. In fact, they only made the opera-tor think I was a pro. So, he set the buck setting to "annihilate." He pushed the button and in less than two seconds it was, "Houston, we have lift off!" I may not have won the prize for the longest ride, but I surely did for the longest flight!

Back to the drawing board.

My transformation then turned to higher education, so I enrolled at Kent State University. One of my professors—a very sophisticated, educated man—always had a pipe in his mouth. Though it was never lit in class, it made an impression on me. I thought *That's what I need, a pipe*. So, there was the "new" Ron: bell-bottom jeans with a cowboy hat perched atop my afro...smok-ing a pipe.

Now do you believe me when I say, "I was a mess"? If you would've known me back then, I'm sure you would've never bought this book! But that was the B.C. me.

I say all this for one purpose: look how far I've bloomed. A life that was once purposeless is now purposeful. God has brought me from being a depressed, despondent, and discouraged young man to a man who is dependently wealthy in Him. I bloomed enough to attract the rarest of birds to pollinate—my lovely bride of over thirty years—and to have all our family saved and in love with Jesus. Some even serve with us in the ministry. That's some real fruit.

And I thank God for it every single day.

THE PATH

As you can see from my story, blooming isn't usually instantaneous. It involves this word we all love to hate: process. Process requires change, and nobody likes change (except from a vending machine). The truth about change is: When you hurt so much you have to, when you learn so much you want to, and when you know so much you can, then you'll change. If that's a little too much to digest, then here's another way to say it:

 B.B.: When the pain of staying the same grows greater than the pain of change, transformation will happen.

I'm a firm believer that God is constantly preparing us for what He has prepared for us. However, because we love our comfort, we often resist or even refuse this preparation time. Comfort is comforting (duh!), but it's really dangerous. In the end, comfort is a shield that keeps us from feeling the pain of staying at the same place in life. I like to say it like this:

Comfort is the advocate to "average."

If your adversary can keep you comfortable, he can keep you average. Why is this? Because he knows that if you ever discover your purpose and destiny, you'll be dangerous. What you already know will keep you from what you need to know to birth your destiny. Read that again. Get it on the inside of you. Now make it personal:

"What I already know will keep me from what I need to know in order to birth my ultimate destiny!"

You can grow with what you know but to bloom beyond where you are now, you're going to have to know more than you do now. If this one truth becomes truly ignited on the inside of you, it will be worth a thousand times what you paid for this book.

WHAT'S INSIDE

There's another you, inside of you, just waiting to blossom. There's another you bursting to bear fruit. You know it's true. You've had dreams, visions, and a "knowing" on the inside that there's more. It's time to start the process.

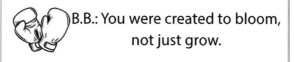

B.B.: You were created to bloom, not just grow.

I've always heard that there are two ways to get to the top of an oak tree: climb the tree or set on an acorn. You see, there are no shortcuts to maturity. Just like the acorn which develops into a beautiful oak tree, it takes time to grow into adulthood. The development of Christ-like character cannot be rushed. Spiritual growth, like physical growth, takes time.

In the same way, fruit doesn't mature and ripen overnight. The same is true for the fruit of the Spirit. Any farmer will tell you that if you try to ripen fruit quickly, it loses its flavor.

Tomatoes are a perfect example. In America, tomatoes are usually picked un-ripened so they won't bruise during shipping. Then, before they are sold, these green tomatoes are sprayed with CO_2 gas which turns them instantly red. Yes, gassed tomatoes are edible, but their flavor is no match to a vine-ripened tomato that slowly matures.

In John 15:5, Jesus used this same analogy, describing Himself as the vine and us the branches. His life flowing into us is a process to make us more like Him. When it does we produce "much fruit."

What's standing in your way from producing this type of fruit? Is it anger? Addictions? Issues from your past? Or maybe just laziness. Whatever it is, I can assure you that it's not worth keeping you from blooming. Do you need professional help? Then get it! Do you need to grow more in commitment to your wife, family, church? Then do it! Take whatever steps you need to start the sap from the true vine (Jesus) to freely flow through you.

Which version of you are you ready for? Say this with me:

"Good, better, or best. Never let it rest; until your good is better, and your better is best."

"Average" grows; ultimate living blooms, blossoms, and produces much fruit. Do you want to defeat the enemy called average? Do more than grow…

…Bloom.

CHAPTER 9

DO MORE THAN CO-EXIST
...RECONCILE

I ONCE HEARD of a young girl who grew up on a beautiful cherry orchard just outside Traverse City, Michigan. She had a great life, but during her teen years, her parents tended to over-react to her nose ring, music choices, friend selection, and style of dress. Every time she was grounded, the young teen seethed inside, "I hate you," toward her old-fashioned parents. Finally, she'd had enough. It was time to act on a plan which had run through her mind countless times before.

The young girl ran away from home.

Where could she go that her parents wouldn't find her? California? Florida? Both of those were too obvious. The best place, in her mind, was a mere four-hour drive away: Detroit. Traverse City newspapers always reported, in lurid detail, the gang activity, drugs, and violence there. It seemed to be the perfect place to escape.

On her second day there, the young girl met a man who drove the biggest car she'd ever seen. This total stranger was nice enough to offer her a ride, buy her lunch, and provide her living arrangements. He also provided some pills which produced a feeling she had never felt before. She quickly concluded that her parents were indeed keeping her from all the fun. This was the right decision.

A month went by, then another, then another. Finally, one year—a year of living in a penthouse with all its perks—had passed. Seeing her picture printed on a "Have you seen this child?" poster once posed a brief scare. But now, with her blond hair, body-piercings, and new makeup, no one would mistake her for a child. Occasionally, she thought about the folks back home. Their lives seemed so boring and provincial, it was hard to imagine she had actually lived there. This was her new life.

This was the good life.

The man with the big car—whom she called "boss"—taught her a few things that men like, which she became proficient in performing. Being underage, men paid a premium for her services. But it didn't last long. After another year, things drastically changed.

At the first sign of an illness, "boss" changed his attitude. "These days, we can't mess around with diseases," he growled. And just like that, the good life came to a screeching halt. Instead of the penthouse, now this tattered young lady was on the street, without a penny to her name.

Desperate for money, she turned a couple of tricks a night, but without much pay. All of her earnings supported her new found drug addiction. When the brutal Michigan winter came, she found herself sleeping on metal grates outside big department stores. But does she really sleep? Can a young teenaged girl, alone on the streets of downtown Detroit, ever let her guard down?

Now this "woman of the world" suddenly realized who she really was: a little girl lost in a cold, big, frightening city. She was hungry, abandoned, and needed a fix. It was all she could do to stay warm underneath the newspapers piled atop her coat. Suddenly, a single image flashed across her memory—a May day in Traverse City with a million cherry trees in bloom. Questions and guilt painfully bombarded her mind: Why did I leave? Where do I go now? What happened to the "good life?"

It was time to go home.

Two calls back home resulted in two straight connections with the answering machine. Embarrassed as to what to say, she hung up. Then, a third call. Same results...except this time, she bravely says, "Dad, Mom, it's me. I was wondering if I could come home. I'll catch the bus up your way. It arrives at midnight tomorrow night. If you're not there, I'll just keep going to Canada."

The seven-hour bus ride only produced more conflicting thoughts. Was her plan flawed from the beginning? What if her parents were out of town? Do they even know she's coming home? Should she have waited another day? Even if they are home, have they written her off as dead?

As the bus rolled on, tiny snowflakes accumulated on the road. A deer crossing the road reminds her how dark it is here at night. Signs posting mileage to Traverse City confirmed the bus was getting closer and closer. Was she ready to see the ones she walked out on just a few months earlier? Will they notice the tobacco stains on her fingertips and bags under her eyes? What will they say? What will she say?

The trip allowed time to rehearse her speech over and over,

"Daddy, I'm so sorry. I know I was wrong. It's not your fault, it's mine. Daddy, can you forgive me?" Asking forgiveness wasn't something she was accustomed to.

Finally, the moment of truth. Stopping at the Traverse City station, the driver announced, "Fifteen minutes, folks. That's all the time we have here." Fifteen minutes to decide her fate. Sheepishly, she made her way off the bus into the unknown.

Walking into the terminal, not one of the thousand scenarios played in her mind could've prepared her for what awaited. There, amongst the concrete walls and plastic chairs, stood a group of over forty family members, all wearing party hats and blowing noisemakers! Behind her parents and the sea of brothers, sisters, aunts, uncles, grandmother, and even a great-grandmother read a sign, "Welcome home!"

From the crowd of well-wishers breaks one to the front of her line: her father. Through an ocean of tears she begins her memorized speech: "Dad, I'm sorry. I know..." He interrupts, "Hush, child. We've got no time for that. No time for apologies. You'll be late for the party." "Party?" she asks. "Yes," continues her father, "a banquet's waiting for you at home."

I can identify with this story as I, too, was a child who ran away from home. Like this teenaged girl, I came to my senses and wanted to go home. Oh, yes, my family met me at the airport, but what happened after all the emotion wore off was a very different story.

You see, we were your very "average" family. What that meant was, even though we were all reunited back in the same house, our relationship with each other was still miles apart. We co-existed...

...but we didn't reconcile. (That came later with the introduction of Jesus to our family.)

SOMETHING'S WRONG

In over thirty years of counseling married couples, I've come to realize one painful fact: Far too many people go through life co-existing. How many marriages "stay together" just for the kids' sake? That's not living; that's co-existing. And, it's a sure sign of an average life.

Could the story of the teenage girl really be true? Is it possible to go through such hurt, betrayal, deceitfulness, lack of respect, etc., and be able to put the relationships back together? Not in an "average" family. But in a family committed to an extraordinary life, yes, it is possible!

 B.B.: Breaking the barrier of average requires reconciliation.

And to be stronger and healthier than before.

To reconcile means, "to reestablish, to resolve, or to regain friendship by pleasant behavior." By looking at these definitions, how would classify your life? Do you coexist and cohabitate, or are you a reconciler?

The Bible addresses this subject. Romans 12:18 says:

> *"If it is possible, as much as depends on you, live peaceably with all men."*

And 1 Peter 3:11 says:

"...Do not merely desire peaceful relations with God, your fellowmen, and with yourself, but pursue, go after them!"

(AMPC)

In a time when peaceful relationships are fading away, even to the brink of extinction, adhering to these scriptures like never before is a necessity. Average marriages, even among Christians, are failing at a record rate. Broken homes and families are the new "norm." Friend, something is desperately wrong. It's time to stop living an average life.

It's time to step up, reconcile broken and wounded relationships, and live the life God has provided.

LIVING BLESSED

Some of my greatest growth opportunities occurred during some of my hardest relationship trials. Because I strive to reconcile and keep peace, God has a way of using those people who can grate on me like sandpaper to knock off all the pits and bumps in my own life. It's the power of reconciliation.

As a believer in Jesus Christ, you must let your light shine in the darkness. Your light is your faith, your belief, *and* your corresponding behavior. For some reason, many Christians seem to ignore the last step.

When it comes to relationships, you can act just like the world and push everyone to the back of the line. Even worse, you can manipulate people with your words and emotions—or completely shove them out of your life altogether with your words and/or actions. You have complete permission to be you.

However, if that version of "you" is hurtful to others, don't look for many others to be in your life. That's how "average" (or below average) people behave.

But, that's not you.

Because your behavior emulates the Jesus in you, you're a reconciler. Instead of shunning others, you go the extra mile to help them find their place. You open doors of communication so that differences can be expressed and peace brought to a situation. You walk in self-control and understand that love covers a multitude of sins. Reconcilers never return evil for evil, but rather forgive so that God's love is seen and experienced. Like the Scripture says, you pursue peaceful relationships.

Of course, you might say, "Ron, you don't know how others have hurt me or what they've done to my family." I get it. But I'm probably right in guessing they haven't crucified you, right? Well, that's exactly what happened to Jesus. Yet, as He hung on the cross, the ultimate reconciler asked His Heavenly Father to forgive those who wrongfully killed Him, because they had no idea what they were doing. (See Luke 2:34.)

You have that very same internal capacity.

There was a time in our life when Donna's family closed the door of relationship in our face. Even worse, it was at a time when we needed their support and friendship the most. Donna's mother had recently died plus we were in the midst of making some radical decisions for our daughter's well-being. Our mistake was not including Donna's family in these decisions. Without any notice, WHAM, the doors were slammed. We were completely cut off, including holiday family get-togethers.

We had a decision to make. Were we going to be the "average" family and hold a grudge, or were we going to live above that ceiling and reconcile? Thankfully, we chose the high road. We chose to break the barrier of average.

And our decision paid big dividends.

Jesus said, "*Blessed* are the peacemakers, for they shall be called sons of God." (Matthew 5:9, italics added.) Does your enemy want you blessed? Is it his desire for you to be called a child of God? Of course not. What's his plan? To keep you average. But, there is a better way. It's called reconciliation.

And it's quickly becoming part of your life.

HOW DOES IT WORK?

So, what are the steps to reconciliation? How can you restore those relationships to how they once were, or even better? What Christ-like behavior is required? Here are few pointers:

> **Develop caring listening skills**. In an "average" relationship, you care more about what you have to say than hearing what the other person is saying. Reconciling is completely different. Learn to truly hear what others are saying.
>
> **Own how you feel**. "Average" people hardly ever express their real feelings in any situation. That's one reason they live "average" lives. A large part of reconciliation is open communication. Owning what you feel, and sharing it, is one of the quickest ways to rebuilding relationships. When sharing feelings, completely avoid blaming. Instead, focus on talking about the feelings of "me" and "I."
>
> **Establish boundaries**. Without boundaries, you have no ownership of your life. Without

boundaries, even good-hearted people will often go further than you may like in order to control you. Establish boundaries and then maintain them. They are there to protect you. In my life, the circles of closeness are like rings on a bullseye. Godly character demands love and peace. The further outside of these someone lives, the farther outside of my inner circle they become.

Donna and I live on a five-acre fenced property. Our neighbor's properties are fenced, too. It communicates, "You, your animals, equipment, etc. can come this far, but any further requires permission." Some of our neighbors go the extra mile, posting signs that say, "Keep out. Private property." That doesn't offend me. I haven't had one sleepless night over it. Why? Because we expect people to place borders on their property. So, why are we often offended when others place boundaries on their life?

We shouldn't be.

People pay big dollars for surveyors to confirm and secure their property boundaries. The question is, why do you care more about a piece of property than your own personal life? Again, you shouldn't. Much like property borders, proper personal boundaries keep people from overstepping their bounds and trespassing into your garden.

I have the amazing opportunity to sit on the board of our township, Parrish, Florida. Recently, I witnessed the most influential man in our area callously run all over several other people, me included. He crossed the boundary. Honestly, I was so hurt that I wanted to step down from my position—after I busted his chops, of course! But, I chose to live above "average" and to reconcile instead of coexisting.

After our next meeting, I asked if I could speak with him privately. I told him what I had witnessed from my vantage point and what I was feeling. He surprised me by saying that I was right! He admitted to being very short-sighted in this regard and didn't even know he was hurting others. He was very sincere, and I believed him. Then, he threw me a zinger.

Before we ended our conversation, this man asked if I would keep him accountable in that area. Knowing the power of boundaries, I agreed—but only to the degree I felt he was listening and acting on what I told him. He was extremely thankful. Since that time, I've watched this man turn a major corner in his interactions with others. It's the power of listening, sharing your feelings, and knowing boundaries. In the end, reconciliation happened before anything was even broken.

What if I would've acted like an "average" person? I would have stepped down from my position and retaliated by justifying my absence to the others this man had abused. Believe me, I had enough ammunition and poison to really hurt him, but I chose not to fall victim to an "average" life.

Today, this man continues to be an integral, meaningful, and necessary leader in our community. Our friendship has deepened, which has been a blessing to my life. Most importantly, he is ever closer to receiving Jesus as his Lord—which is the ultimate reconciliation.

All of this would have been aborted by the enemy called "average."

AN OPEN DOOR

Does this type of rebuilding sound like it's out of your grasp? Think again. The Bible says that every Believer—including you—has the ministry of reconciliation. (See 2 Corinthians 5:18.) Yes, this scripture is talking about reconciling sinners to Christ, but have you ever tried to win someone to Jesus that you were at odds with? It doesn't work.

During our time of discord, I remember Donna talking about her family on one occasion: "Whenever I received a discouraging letter from one of my family members, it would tear me apart. I'd cry, get angry, and think of something to say in rebuttal. Then, I'd sit and write a letter, asking their forgiveness for whatever I'd done to hurt them so badly. Years went by with little or no responses...until one day.

Never will I forget the day my sister unexpectedly showed up at our front door. She looked at me and said, 'Donna, I have cancer.' Because of my responses over the years, the door was wide open for me to pray for her. Our relationship was reconciled."

In case you're wondering, God completely healed Donna's sister of cancer! Now, they enjoy a wonderful relationship, to the point of being best friends.

That open door is available for you today. Make the decision to reconcile. Refuse to allow your enemy to destroy your family, your friends, your church, your ministry, etc. Is there someone you need to forgive? Recognize that battle is not one of flesh and blood but a spiritual battle that Jesus has already won.

Do you want to break the barrier of average? Stop only coexisting. Take the next step.

Reconcile.

CHAPTER 10

DO MORE THAN SPEND...INVEST

LET'S START THIS chapter with a truth that could change your entire perspective on budgeting. Are you ready?

 B.B.: What you don't value, you spend. What you value, you invest.

Spending and investing, even though lumped into the same category, are hardly the same. Spending is usually a value-to-value exchange. Do you want a gallon of milk? Then you pay four dollars. You spend an hour of your labor in exchange for a wage. If you paint a beautiful picture, you sell it for hundreds of dollars. Spending = value-to-value.

Investing is completely different. Because it's not usually based on value-to-value, investing doesn't always produce the same rapid return as spending. There are times when investments don't pan out. However, there are times when the return far exceeds the investment.

When you hear terms like "spending" and "investing," you immediately think of money. But, there are more currencies of life—time, talent, treasure—which can be included as well.

Take the day I wrote this chapter as an example. I was in Hiawassee, Georgia, camping for a week with my awesome grandson, Israel. Some people would say that I was "spending time with Israel." Not true. I wasn't spending—I was investing. What's the difference? I'm looking for a return on my investment. We had a blast that week, but my approach was ROI (return on investment) oriented. What's the difference? I didn't just spend time with him, I invested it. The focus was on Israel and his destiny. And I'm sure the returns will be seen for years to come.

"Average" people spend. Those who live the abundant life invest. Just think how radically different families, marriages, ministries, and work places could be if people had a paradigm shift from spending to investing. They would all go from average to abundant.

That's the life you're heading towards.

THE THREE "T'S"

Spending is easy. Investing requires more wisdom, discernment, patience, and faith. The more you develop these attributes, the greater the return on your investment. Developing a pattern of God-directed investing produces an abundant, purpose-filled, rich, and satisfying life.

Earlier I mentioned three different currencies in the economy of life: time, talent, and treasure. Let's look at each of these in a bit more detail.

TIME

A philosophy professor stood before his class with some items in front of him. When the class began, he wordlessly picked up a very large, empty mayonnaise jar and proceeded to fill it with golf balls. He then asked the students, "Is the jar full?" They agreed that it was. So, he continued.

Picking up a box of pebbles, the professor poured them into the jar, giving it a light shake. The pebbles settled in the open areas between the golf balls. He then asked the students again, "Is the jar full?" They agreed it was. The experiment continued.

Next was a box of sand. Poured into the jar, the sand found its way into the open spaces. The students were asked once again, "Is the jar full?" They responded with a unanimous, "Yes." Much to their surprise, there was still one more step.

The professor then produced two cups of coffee from under the table and emptied the entire contents into the jar. As the students laughed, again they were faced with the question, "Now, is it full?" Their laughter subsided, and the professor began explaining the thought behind his experiment.

"I want you to realize that this jar represents your life. The golf balls are important things like God, your family, children, health, relationships, and favorite passions. These are the things that, if you lost everything, would still make your life full. The pebbles are other things that matter to you. Your job, house, car, etc. The sand represents the small things in life that are important but not essential. Now, notice something. What would happen if you put the sand in first? There wouldn't be room for the pebbles or golf balls. The same goes for life.

If you spend all your time and energy on small stuff, you'll never have room for the things that are important. Pay attention to the things that are critical to your happiness. Play with your children. Take time for medical checkups. Take your spouse out to dinner. Maybe even play another eighteen holes of golf. There will always be time to clean the house and fix the disposal!

Take care of the golf balls—the things that really matter—first. Set your priorities. The rest is just sand."

After his explanation, one of the students raised her hand and inquired, "Sir, what does the coffee represent?" The professor smiled. "I'm glad you asked. It just goes to show that no matter how full your life may seem, there's always room for a couple of cups of coffee with a friend."

Let's break that down to where you live.

If you're a typical American, you'll spend an average of six months sitting at stoplights, eight months opening junk mail, one year looking for misplaced objects, two years unsuccessfully returning phone calls, four years doing housework, five years waiting in line, and six years eating. Plus, a recent Nielsen Company audience report reveals that adults in the United States spent ten hours and thirty-nine minutes each day consuming media. That's almost thirty-five years!

The point is simple: Invest your time wisely.

 B.B.: More time is wasted in minutes than hours.

The bucket with a small hole in the bottom will be just as empty as the one deliberately kicked over. Plug the holes that drain your time. Pray David's prayer from Psalms 90:12. Ask God to teach you how to number your days, that you may gain a heart of wisdom. Number your days, and steward your time accordingly.

TALENT

When you hear the word "talent," you usually think of a certain ability or aptitude one possesses. While this is true, the Bible has many words which can be interchanged with "talent." They are:

- *Shohad*: a gift to avert punishment; a bribe.
- *Minha:* a propitiatory gift; to pay tribute.
- *Nasa':* to raise, as in funds for a gift.
- *Natan:* a gratuity; a gift of thankfulness.
- *Didomi:* a special gift or endowment for the work of the ministry.

I want you to know something: You are very talented! Not just in your physical and motor-skill talents but in your ability to *shohad,* avoid the punisher; to *minha,* give God glory and honor others; to *nasa',* attract resources; to *natan,* be one who praises God and encourages others. And most importantly, know you are *didomi,* talented to be a special gift for the work of the ministry.

It's time to invest in yourself.

Seeing that you are so talented, look how God's Word talks about you:

> ***"Do not neglect the gift that is in you ... "***

1 Timothy 4:14

"Therefore I remind you to stir up the gift of God which is in you through the laying on of my hands."

2 Timothy 1:6

"As each one has received a gift, minister it to one another, as good stewards of the manifold grace of God."

Peter 4:10

Again, you are full of talents. Recognize them. Walk in them. Develop them. The Bible says God gives seed to the sower. (See 2 Corinthians 9:10.) That's you, the sower! Don't just spend these great gifts and talents; invest them. God is looking for a return on His investment in you and through you.

TREASURE

You are mandated by God to steward two kinds of treasure: heavenly and earthly. Let's examine both.

Heavenly In Matthew 6:19-21, Jesus says:

"Do not lay up for yourselves treasures on earth, where moth and rust destroy and where thieves break in and steal; but lay up for yourselves treasures in heaven, where neither moth nor rust destroys and where thieves do not break in and steal. For where your treasure is, there your heart will be also."

The main difference between heavenly and earthly treasures is simple: earthly ones, without exception, will perish. In Matthew 10:41, Jesus talks about receiving a righteous man's reward. He continues, in verse forty-two, to say that if you do something as simple as giving a kid a drink of water you shall by no means lose your reward. It's easy to see two things: God is a rewarder, and there are rewards that you never lose.

It's amazing how even the simplest thing—the least important act done in the name of Christ—never loses its reward. "Average" spends; above average invests! Invest in your heavenly treasures.

Earthly Deuteronomy 8:18-19 says:

"And you shall remember the Lord your God, for it is He who gives you the power to get wealth, that He may establish His covenant which He swore to your fathers, as it is this day. Then it shall be, if you by any means forget the Lord your God, and follow other gods, and serve them and worship them, I testify against you this day that you shall surely perish."

Contrary to popular belief (and some stupid teaching), earthly treasures are not evil. Money isn't evil, the love of it is. (See 1 Timothy 6:10.) The key to earthly treasure is what you seek. Jesus' instructions were to seek first His Kingdom, and everything else will be added to you. (See Matthew 6:33.)

B.B.: When you put God first in everything you do, it tells Him that you have things, things don't have you.

THE ANT KNOWS!

I love the Bible for many reasons. One is it shows God's wit. Proverbs 6:6-8 is a perfect example. Here, God lays out the plan on how to live an above average life when it comes to investing. To do so, you only have to look on the ground. The ground? Yep. See for yourself:

> *"Go to the ant, you sluggard! Consider her ways and be wise, which, having no captain, overseer or ruler, provides her supplies in the summer, and gathers her food in the harvest."*

One Sunday morning as we were preparing to receive our church's tithes and offerings, I said, "Guys, today I brought in a teacher who's going to impart to us concerning wealth. This teacher is highly qualified and brings a distinguished track record. Would you stand to your feet and help me give a warm welcome our guest this morning?"

Then I sat a jar with an ant in it on the pulpit!

Look how the ant is anything but "average." Self-motivated—not "average." Understanding the seasons—not "average." Does what she can, when she can—not "average." Enjoys a season of rest because of her diligence—not "average." Everything about her is above average. It makes me think, *How far above average can you live?*

The sky's the limit.

RISK VS. REWARD

Any investment portfolio has a risk versus reward disclosure. What this simply means is more risk can potentially produce more reward. The same is true in living an above average life.

Are there risks? Absolutely. But they're well worth the potential return. This actual e-mail exchange between a young man in our church and myself proves the point. I've placed it here for your perusal because I think you will be able to relate and be impacted:

> *Hi pastor! I would love to get some insight from you about faith if you've got a moment. My wife and I just sat down and finished our letter to the churches about asking for prayer for us going to YWAM (Youth With A Mission.) On the bottom of the letter, I wanted to include a blog website where (if they are interested) they can visit and see updates about our journey, including updates on what we are learning and what we are doing for His Kingdom.*
>
> *Anyways, all that to say that I've seen this blog in my mind for months and months now. However, tonight I had a 'new' title for it come into my mind: **Risk of Faith**.*
>
> *This title is not so much a battle in my head, but there's something about it that challenges me. I know that we are stepping out and that if this is not of God, then we will fall straight on our faces and probably look pretty dumb to everyone who knows our goal. It's a risk so to speak. The thing is, can faith be termed risky? God knows the outcome; we don't. If we risk stepping out and the only way we are going to stand is by Him, then guess who gets the glory? That's what I want...jaw dropping awe of God's wonder and power.*
>
> *Do you think the phrase, "risk of faith" is anti-Christ?*
>
> *Love you! As always, thank you for your time!*

My response was as follows:

> *I think this might be one we have to have a deeper conversation about. But here's a nutshell version until then.*
>
> *Risk, to me, automatically includes doubt. And true faith is to be w/o doubt. However, there is risk following God. So to answer your question, yes…and, no.*
>
> *Faith has everything to do with trust. If you truly heard from God to go to YWAM, then you are going trusting in His leading. But, what if it doesn't turn out like you thought? Does that mean you took a risk and lost? Or, does it mean that He spoke, and no matter the outcome, you're following Him? Things didn't turn out for Jesus's cousin, John, like he thought it would. He doubted briefly (Luke 7:19) and probably thought, "Geez, I risked everything on Him, and now I'm headed to get my head chopped off!" Jesus sent a soul-shaking message to him: "Blessed is he who is not offended because of me," (Luke 7:23). If John looked at it as risk, well, he'd rolled the dice and lost. If he looked at it as, 'I will follow You no matter the cost,' then I would say John followed Jesus, even unto death.*
>
> *We read about one who had the same question, but decided the other way—Judas.*
>
> *Summary: I don't look at it as risk, I look at it as relationship. No greater love has anyone than he lay down his life for his friends. For me, in following Jesus, things have not always turned out like I thought they would. Yet, I follow. Why? I trust him.*

I love him. And ultimately, His purpose comes forth. (We live life forward, but see it in reverse!) Paul said in Phil 3:8-9, "Yet indeed I also count all things loss for the excellence of the knowledge of Christ Jesus my Lord, for whom I have suffered the loss of all things, and count them as rubbish, that I may gain Christ." What's he saying? "Anything I lost, I let it go and still pursued Christ. And you know what? What I lost was rubbish, what I gained was true wealth!"

Romans 8:28 says, "And we know that all things work together for good to those who love God, to those who are the called according to His purpose."

Love,

Ron

Risk implies that the cause you venture into will hopefully return without a loss. That's exactly the life of Jesus—the ultimate destroyer of average. His cause cost Him His entire life. Would He have come to the earth just for the risk? I don't think so. He knew the reward that awaited his obedience. And He gladly did it.

Investing, in any arena, is risky. The good news is, God is busy accelerating returns in these last days. The Bible describes it as "the plowman overtaking the reaper." (See Amos 9:13.) There will always be a time to plant (invest) and a time to reap (reward). That law will never cease. So, what are you waiting on? Anybody can spend. But the person reaching for a higher life learns to invest—time, talent, and treasure. Do you want to break the barrier called "average?" Then pump the brakes on spending, and put the pedal to the metal on investing.

And watch "average" die.

SELAH

WOW! CAN YOU believe you're already halfway through this book? Stop for a moment and ask yourself, "Why am I reading this book?" If you have a solid answer, then go ahead, hit "play" and keep reading; the best is yet to come. However, if your "why" has grown fuzzy, take a break and read the following. It may help you regain focus.

LIVING ABOVE THE SNAKE LINE

Donna and I love to hike, especially in the mountains—the Blue Ridge, Rockies, Alps, etc. Many of the places we hike and camp have poisonous snakes. Snake bites can be extremely painful and sometimes even deadly. One thing we've learned in our travels is that there's an elevation line above which snakes don't live. Take rattlesnakes for example. Very rarely are they found above sixty-five hundred feet. This border is appropriately called the "snake line."

Let's take the concept from camping in the mountains to

everyday life. You have an enemy, called the devil, who's often referred to as a serpent or snake. He lives to cause you trauma, pain, and death both naturally and spiritually. Even though you live in a fallen world—a world where sometimes bad things happen to good people (even Christians)—you have the power to restrict the enemy's access to your life. That means:

You can live above the snake line!

God has the perfect prescription for living a life far above average. It's called the Bible. His Word is calling you to a life-style of repentance, forgiveness, obedience, and love. Seeing that Paul calls your body a "tent" (See 2 Corinthians 5:1 and 2 Peter 1:13.) It is true: *You can pitch your tent above the snake line.* You can live in the higher elevations of life. That's the place where the God of this universe has designed for you to live.

You can do it. You can pack up your stuff (and purposefully leave some "junk" behind) and head for the high country. You are on your way to living above the snake line. It's the place where "average" cannot be found and God's abundant blessings flow. Are you ready? Then let's keep moving.

The best *is* yet to come.

CHAPTER 11

DO MORE THAN WORK...EXCEL

"AVERAGE" PEOPLE WORK. Those who rise above that stage of life excel in everything they do. They live a life of excellence. No, they're not perfect. Only one person who ever lived was. Excellence is not perfection; it's doing your absolute best—above and beyond what's expected—in every situation.

And it all begins with your perception.

A man watched as three brick layers worked on a new church building. After a bit, he approached them one at a time and asked them about their jobs. Their responses were quite different.

> Man #1: "I'm laying bricks. It's my job. I hate it, but it pays the bills."
>
> Man #2: "I'm building a building. It's my career. I enjoy it."

Man #3: "I'm building a beautiful sanctuary, a place where people will discover God and build beautiful lives together. It's my life. I live for this. I'm paid very well, but I'd do it for free just to see the end result."

Same task. Three completely different approaches. The difference is simple: "Average" makes an objective hard work; excellence makes accomplishing an objective meaningful, fulfilling, and even fun.

When I was a kid, my mom had a great way of showing us three boys how excellence is fun. Of all the chores we had to do, drying the dishes was our least favorite. I think we would've rather drank battery acid! (We prayed for a dishwasher—in the form of a sister—but that never happened.) For years Mom had to put up with us fussing and fighting over who's turn it was to dry dishes. Then, she came up with an idea that changed everything.

Mom started using the silverware to play "pick-up-sticks" with whoever was supposed to dry that night. It was challenging, entertaining, and fun. Now we were disappointed when it *wasn't* our night to dry. She went a step further and wouldn't let us play until we did a good job washing the plates first. Those dishes were spotless! Excellence and fun were now easy.

What changed? The approach. Same job, different tactic, different results. Excellence often requires sacrifice. Seek God for creative ways to make your diligence more enjoyable. Your attitude determines your altitude.

THE CROWN

Excellence isn't automatic. It has to be pursued. You know you're living a life of excellence when you: care more than others think is wise; risk more than others think safe; dream more than others think is practical; and expect more than others think is possible.

There's hardly a better example of these principles in action than in the life of Joseph. If anyone ever lived a rollercoaster life, it was Joseph. But through it all, he maintained a spirit of excellence. Here's a graph of what his life looked like:

- God gave Joseph a dream. ╱

- Joseph told his family what God had revealed to him. ╱╲

- When Joseph's family wanted to kill him, his brother, Judah, saved his life. ╲╱╱

- Joseph is sold into slavery. ╱╲╱╲

- Lands a job in one of Pharaoh's officer's house. ╱╲╱╱

- Thrown in prison when the officer's wife has the hots for him! ╱╲╱╲

- Finds favor with the keeper of the prison; has an encounter with a couple of guys who are being released. ╱╲╱╲╱

- Freed prisoners forget about him; spends two more years in prison. ╱╲╱╲╲

- Brought before Pharaoh, interprets dream, becomes second in command of an entire kingdom. ╱╲╱╲╱

Final outcome: DESTINY! Your excellence for Him builds a crown of glory to the Lord!

If Joseph would have aborted his excellence anywhere during this process—whether up or down—he would have short-circuited his destiny. He had to complete the process. In the end, Joseph saved the same brothers who tried to kill him from famine.

Your life is just like Joseph's—minus some of the extremes I'm sure. No matter where you are in life, your excellence will be tested throughout the entire process. Do not abort it! Strive to make your graph look like Joseph's.

 B.B.: Your crown of glory comes from how you handle trials.

God's continually preparing you for the destiny attached to your life. But destiny doesn't come free. There's a price to pay. That price?

Excellence.

IT'S WORTH IT

The number one excellence to be pursued in an above-average life is the knowledge of Christ. Any other achievement falls short. There's no comparison. In fact, God loves to showcase His excellence through you, His child. The Bible says:

> *"But we have this treasure in earthen vessels, that the excellence of the power may be of God and not of us."*

2 Corinthians 4:7

True excellence comes as you allow Christ to have His way in and through you. It's part of the process known as growing into an abundant life. Again, excellence is not perfection. Being a perfectionist is bondage.

 B.B.: It's not about being *the* best; it's about being *your* best in every area of life.

Whether it's practicing medicine, carpentry, preaching, teaching, parenting, marriage, athletics, or academics, your commitment to excellence will largely determine your results. Mediocrity won't do. As a matter of fact, the word *mediocre* comes from the Latin word "mediocris" which means, "halfway up the mountain." God has a mountain for you to climb. "Average" will only take you half way. For many, the climb is too steep; the effort required is too much. So, they settle. Not you. Don't quit half way up.

The prize is worth the process.

Jerry was a young Starkville, Mississippi boy whose father was a bricklayer. It wasn't uncommon for him and his brothers to help out at their father's job site. Jerry usually stayed on the platform with his dad as his younger brothers threw bricks up, one at a time. Even though it was just laying bricks, Jerry determined to be his best. Little did he know how his commitment to excellence—even in brick laying—would pave the way to an incredible future.

What started as catching bricks turned into catching footballs. The young man's commitment to excellence remained. In the end, San Francisco Forty-Niner, Jerry Rice, became one of the most decorated receivers ever to play in the NFL. Today, he's in the Hall of Fame.

So, what about you? Are you exuding excellence in every area of your life? You don't know? Well, let's take a survey and see. Most people won't even attempt this. They're either too threatened by seeing their score in black and white, or they think they know it all. They love "average." Again, that's not you. You're pushing above mediocrity.

On a scale of one to ten, rate your level of excellence in each of the following areas. (NOTE: If you score less than ten on the first one, don't bother with the rest until you fix that one!)

Honesty	1	2	3	4	5	6	7	8	9	10
Knowledge	1	2	3	4	5	6	7	8	9	10
Relationships Finances	1	2	3	4	5	6	7	8	9	10
Habits	1	2	3	4	5	6	7	8	9	10
Behaviors	1	2	3	4	5	6	7	8	9	10
Attitude	1	2	3	4	5	6	7	8	9	10
Beliefs	1	2	3	4	5	6	7	8	9	10
Speech	1	2	3	4	5	6	7	8	9	10
Planning	1	2	3	4	5	6	7	8	9	10
Organization	1	2	3	4	5	6	7	8	9	10
Appearance	1	2	3	4	5	6	7	8	9	10
Goals	1	2	3	4	5	6	7	8	9	10

Congratulations. Now you know where you stand. You're on your way to excellence. The question is, what is your plan to upgrade the areas that need help? Don't be afraid. Commit to excellence in every area of life. Look at each area and ask yourself, *What would it take to move me from where I am to a ten?* And if you're really serious, ask someone who knows you well to score you. Ask them to be honest, and afterward, thank them…

…No matter how they score you.

DO IT

You've probably heard this before: The rest of your life will be the best of your life. It's true...if you make the changes to better yourself. Don't allow your enemy to talk you out of climbing the mountain all the way to the top. Press on. Take higher ground. Don't grow weary in doing your best. You will reap a harvest if you don't faint.

Keep your mind and thoughts constantly thinking on the right things. Philippians 4:8 provides a great list:

> *"Finally, brothers, whatever is true, whatever is honorable, whatever is just, whatever is pure, whatever is lovely, whatever is commendable, if there is any excellence, if there is anything worthy of praise, think about these things."*

> (ESV)

Pursuit is the proof of desire. Work will get you "average." Excel and God will give you advancement, promotion, and increase. Go on, you can do it! Do you want to destroy the barrier of average? Do more than work...

...Excel.

CHAPTER 12

DO MORE THAN
CONSIDER...COMMIT

IF THERE'S ONE word every "average" person hates, it's the word "commitment." As a matter of fact, most "average" people despise that word. The thought of pursuing something wholeheartedly, with no contingency plan, scares them to death. Maybe that's why they live an "average" life!

Commitment simply means being one hundred percent sold out to something, be it a person, cause, goal, etc. It's going "all in" without holding anything back or keeping anything in reserve. Sounds scary, doesn't it? It is! That's what makes is such a huge part of living above "average."

Spanish explorer, Hernando Cortez, was anything but average. On April 21, 1519, he, along with only six hundred men, sailed into the harbor of Vera Cruz, Mexico. Nearly two years later, his vastly outnumbered army defeated Montezuma along with all the Aztec Empire warriors. Cortez was now the conqueror of all Mexico. How was such an incredible feat accomplished, when two prior expeditions failed to even establish a colony on Mexican soil?

Here's the secret.

From the beginning, Cortez knew that he and his men faced incredible odds. The road before them was undoubtedly dangerous and difficult. He also realized that somewhere during this journey, his men would be tempted to abandon their quest and return to Spain. So, he took action.

As soon as the troops came ashore and unloaded their provisions, Cortez commanded the men, "Burn the ships!" All six-hundred watched as the entire fleet of eleven vessels burned and sank. At that moment, there was no turning back. Nothing lay behind them except an empty ocean. Now there were only two options: conquer or die.

Commitment paid off.

The biblical account of Ruth is another great example of relentless commitment. Ruth was a young woman who understood commitment and thus lived an extraordinary life. In the midst of a major life decision, Ruth told her mother-in-law:

> *"...Do not urge me to leave you or turn back from following you; for where you go, I will go, and where you lodge, I will lodge. Your people shall be my people, and your God, my God. Where you die, I will die, and there I will be buried. Thus may the Lord do to me, and worse, if anything but death parts you and me."*

> Ruth 1:16-17 (NASB)

Talk about commitment. That's the kind God admires...one that sets its course and never turns back.

WHAT IT'S NOT

On your way up to a higher place in life, let me give you a warning on this subject: Commitment cannot be confused with other closely related things such as enjoyment, interests, or involvement. Since they are often mistaken for commitment, let's take a closer look at each one.

> **Enjoyment.** When you do something you enjoy, it's called enjoyment. (That's deep, I know!) Rarely does commitment and enjoyment intersect. Confusing the two usually creates problems.

Take marriage for instance. When you're in a season where you enjoy being married, it's easy to be committed. But when you go through a storm or marital battle, it's a completely different animal. The temptation to quit and walk out raises its ugly head. To weather the storm isn't fun, but commitment will see you through.

In those times of struggle, Donna and I committed to each other never to let the "D" word come up in conversation. "Murder?" Sometimes, but never divorce! We are committed to one another—forever. And we've conquered.

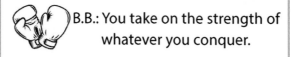 B.B.: You take on the strength of whatever you conquer.

Don't get me wrong. I'm in no way against enjoying life. Are you kidding? Donna and I live life to its fullest every single day. We work, play, adventure, and laugh more than any couple I know. That's what this book is all about: living a life far above your expectations. Just know that somewhere along the trail—many times along the trail—your commitment will be put to the test. Will you be ready? Understanding the difference between enjoyment and commitment will help prepare you.

Interest. One of my favorite quotes concerning commitment is this: "There's a difference between interest and commitment. When you're interested in doing something, you do it only when circumstance permit. When you're committed to something, you accept no excuses, only results." -Author unknown

One of the world's most beloved missionaries, David Livingston, once received a note from a missionary society. It read, "Have you found a good road to where you are? If so, we want to know how to send other men to join you." Livingstone responded, "If you have men who will come only if they know there is a good road, I don't want them. I want men who will come if there is no road at all!"

There's nothing wrong with taking an interest in things, people, causes, etc. But don't stop there. "Average" people never go any further. To break that barrier, turn your interest into a commitment, and watch God put His blessing all over it.

Involvement. Ask anyone who was in a divorce court today and they'll tell you: "Just because you're involved in something does not mean you're committed to it." Involvement and commitment are two totally different things.

Perhaps a breakfast table provides the best example of the two. The next time you set down for a hearty egg and bacon breakfast, let it be a lesson. The hen? She's *involved* in this meal. The pig? That sucker's *committed*! Okay, it may be a bad example, but you get the point. As a leader, I love working with people who are committed. And I often loathe working with people who are just involved.

Involvement is frequently governed by things like convenience, comfort, and preference. In a proper setting, these things are great. But, I'd be concerned if the U.S. military were driven by these. To prove my point, here's a small excerpt from the Navy Seal Creed:

"My Trident is a symbol of honor and heritage. Bestowed upon me by the heroes that have gone before, it embodies the trust of those I have sworn to protect. By wearing the Trident I accept the responsibility of my chosen profession and way of life. It is a privilege that I must earn every day.

My loyalty to country and team is beyond reproach. I humbly serve as a guardian to my fellow Americans always ready to defend those who are unable to defend themselves."

Another section says: "I will never quit. I persevere and thrive on adversity. My nation expects me to be physically harder and mentally stronger than my enemies. If knocked down, I will get back up, every time. I will draw on every remaining ounce of strength to protect my teammates and to accomplish our mission. I am never out of the fight."

Wow! When you commit rather than getting involved in your marriage, family, church, career, health, etc., you will see dividends being paid, and "average" being crushed.

JUMP IN

Leadership guru, John Maxwell, wrote in his book, *Be a People Person*, "Until I am committed, there is a hesitancy, a chance to draw back. But the moment I definitely commit myself, then God moves also, and a whole stream of events erupt. All manner of unforeseen incidents, meetings, persons, and material assistance which I could never have dreamed would come my way begin to flow toward me—the moment I make a commitment."

Friend, if for no other reason, that's reason enough to pursue commitment.

Of all Jesus' disciples, you have to love Peter. Yes, he made some very stupid decisions and wasn't as consistent as he should've been (sounds a lot like you and me, right?), but when it came down it, Peter was committed to His Lord.

John Chapter 21 records an incident after Jesus had resurrected from the dead. After some days, Peter, a fisherman before Jesus called him to be a disciple, decided to go back to what he knew—fishing. He tells the other disciples, "Guys, Jesus is gone. I'm going back to fishing." They all agreed to go with him. Together, they found a boat and set out to the sea. There was only one problem.

They caught nothing all night.

Early the next morning, Jesus was standing on the shore, but the disciples didn't realize it was Him. He called out to them, "Friends, haven't you any fish?" "No," they answered. He then said, "Throw your net on the right side of the boat and you will find some." The disciples obeyed and they were unable to haul in the net due to the large number of fish. At that moment, John yelled to Peter, "It's the Lord!" That's all it took.

Without any hesitation, Peter wrapped his outer garment around him, jumped in the water, and took off for the shore.

You've gotta love this guy. As soon as he realizes Jesus is on the shore, he immediately jumps into the water and starts swimming for all he's worth. He never stops to calculate the speed of the boat. Maybe it was faster to row. At that point and time, it didn't matter. All Peter knew was that Jesus was ahead.

That's commitment.

The rest of the story? Peter's commitment paid big dividends. In the end, Jesus wound up giving him a very clear, prophetic direction concerning his life. Many years later, when Peter was in line to be beheaded, those words came flying back into his mind, assuring Peter that his life wasn't over, and he wasn't going to die.

Once again, commitment paid off.

WHAT ABOUT YOU?

It's no secret that God hates wishy-washiness. He's not a fan of fence-sitters, and He isn't pleased by people who can never make up their minds. You know, the ones who forever weigh their options and can never settle on a course of action. In other words:

God's not a fan of "average."

So, let me ask you, are you sold out for God? Are you determined to seek after Him with all your heart, soul, mind, and strength? Are you hot, cold, or disgustingly lukewarm? Have you counted the cost of following Jesus, or are you trying to have it both ways—one foot in the Kingdom, the other in the world? If you are, I can tell you that you're miserable! I don't think there's anything worse than trying to serve God, the world, and yourself all at the same time. Jesus said that it's better to be a whole-hearted pagan. At least there's hope for your salvation. (See Revelation 3:15-16.)

There was a time when Jesus even questioned His own disciples' commitment to Him. John 6:66-68 records it:

> *"From this time many of his disciples turned back and no longer followed him. 'You do not want to leave too, do you?' Jesus asked the Twelve. Simon Peter answered him, 'Lord, to whom shall we go? You have the words of eternal life.'"*

> (NIV)

Now, do you see why "average" people hate commitment? The average follower of Jesus enjoys life, but when the water gets hot, they don't jump in, they jump out!

Let me end this chapter with a statement written by a young African pastor. This was found amongst his papers after he was martyred:

> *"I'm a part of the fellowship of the unashamed. The die has been cast. I have stepped over the line. The decision has been made. I'm a disciple of His and I won't look back, let up, slow down, back away, or be still.*

> *My past is redeemed. My present makes sense. My future is secure. I'm done and finished with low living, sight walking, small planning, smooth knees, colorless dreams, tamed visions, mundane talking, cheap living, and dwarfed goals.*

> *I no longer need preeminence, prosperity, position,*

promotions, plaudits, or popularity. I don't have to be right, or first, or tops, or recognized, or praised, or rewarded. I live by faith, lean on His presence, walk by patience, lift by prayer, and labor by Holy Spirit power.

My face is set. My gait is fast. My goal is heaven. My road may be narrow, my way rough, my companions few, but my guide is reliable and my mission is clear.

I will not be bought, compromised, detoured, lured away, turned back, deluded or delayed. I will not flinch in the face of sacrifice or hesitate in the presence of the adversary. I will not negotiate at the table of the enemy, ponder at the pool of popularity, or meander in the maze of mediocrity. I won't give up, shut up, or let up until I have stayed up, stored up, prayed up, paid up, and preached up for the cause of Christ.

I am a disciple of Jesus. I must give until I drop, preach until all know, and work until He comes. And when He does come for His own, He'll have no problems recognizing me. My colors will be clear!"

It's been said that "Commitment in the face of conflict produces character." It's true. When the going gets tough, the tough get going by hanging in there, no matter the cost. Do you want to destroy the barrier of average in your life? Then stop considering...

...Commit.

CHAPTER 13

DO MORE THAN
FORGIVE...FORGET

COMMITMENT, NOW FOLLOWED by forgetting things and people you've already forgiven. Ouch! Can you now see why we took a little Selah moment? Yes, these two chapters are tough but completely necessary for you to break through the barrier of "average." You can do it. Just hang on for the ride.

Did you ever hear the story about the man with a horrible memory? We'll call him John. One day, John ran into a friend, Bill, whom he hadn't seen in a long time. He greeted him and said, "Bill, do you remember what a bad memory I used to have?" Bill answered, "Yes, I certainly do." "Well," John replied, "it's not bad any longer. I went to a seminar that taught me how to remember things. Now I have a wonderful memory." Bill said, "That's great. What was the name of the seminar?" "Well," said John, "Wait a minute. My wife went with me. I'll ask her."

John turned to his wife, who was standing nearby. He

started to say something, then he looked back at Bill and asked, "What's that flower with a long stem and thorns?" "Do you mean a rose?" Bill replied. "Yeah, thanks," said John. Then he turned back to his wife, "Hey, Rose. What's the name of that seminar we attended?"

As humorous as this little story is, this isn't the type of forgetting I'm talking about. This chapter isn't about forgetting things you should remember but rather forgetting those things that hold you back.

In Philippians 3:13, Paul instructs us to forget those things which are behind and to press toward the things God has for us. He calls it the "upward call of God in Christ Jesus." I know that as we grow older, forgetfulness is not something we cherish. But according to this scripture, there is a forgetfulness that God loves. It's when we forget the stuff in our rearview mirror.

Sometimes, that's much easier said than done.

Let me ask you a question. Have you ever been burned by someone? Okay, if you're more than three years old, the answer is most probably, "Yes!" Maybe numerous times.

Several years ago, Donna and I were approached with an opportunity from a well-known and respected investor. He was looking to purchase tracks of land for housing developments. This particular land was already approved by the city, but no one was pursuing it. Between the buying volume and the ability to purchase materials pre-construction, our return on investment was amazing—somewhere around fifty percent. It was a "no brainer." Or, so we thought.

This deal was such a sure bet that Donna and I broke one of our cardinal rules: We didn't pray about it! And, we didn't use discernment. In the end, it cost us dearly.

This so-called "investor" absconded with $100,000 of our

money, along with millions of other people's money. It was our entire life savings up to that point. We spent years in the court system trying to recoup our investment. After winning the first case, the company this guy worked for appealed. When it was evident they were going to lose, they filed for bankruptcy, ending all hope of us receiving any monies.

I was devastated.

Here's what I learned: Money is probably the least invasive loss anyone can experience. Relationships are the most invasive.

Not too long ago, we asked our longtime friends if their son could stay at our house while we were away. They agreed. We felt safe knowing someone we had known for years was going to be there. However, while he was there he stole things from our house worth thousands of dollars. We obviously weren't as safe as we thought!

The stuff wasn't nearly as difficult to deal with as the wound to the relationship. This young man still has no idea that we know. Donna and I are keeping our love towards him in tact until we can reach the point of a healthy confrontation. In the meantime, we've made the decision to live with ourselves, and his family, as though it never happened. Why?

Because that's exactly what God did for us.

FORGETFULNESS THAT HEALS

Do you know what unforgiveness looks like? Of course you do. You—like everyone else—has a history with it. We've all experienced it, either from us towards others or from others towards us. Either way, it's nasty, ugly, and incredibly divisive. But, there's another side of this coin: You most definitely know what forgiveness looks like, as well.

When we finally accepted the fact that we lost all our savings, I did what I knew to do. I went before the Lord, sobbed, cried, was broken, and then cleansed all the unforgiveness from my heart. But, something remained. I still *remembered* how this guy took advantage of us. Every time that wound started to heal, I ripped it open again by replaying what happened. Not only was I still wounded, everyone around me knew it.

I was living a below-average life.

I once heard of a wonderful lady who was brutally raped. It was an awful experience, one that no human being should ever be forced to endure. After a while, this lady found it in herself to forgive the man who violated her.

About six months later, she came across a friend who knew about the incident. Her friend was shocked at how much this lady had changed. Not only was she no longer grieving, she was absolutely radiant. Her friend said, "I'm shocked. You look and sound so good. I never expected to see you this happy, especially this soon. What happened?" The woman replied "Oh, that's easy. I made up my mind that while this man may have raped me once, he's not going to continue to rape me for the rest of my life!"

 B.B.: To forgive is one thing; to forget is an entirely different level of living.

Wow!

Not exercising forgiveness all the way to forgetfulness is bondage. Yes, you may have forgiven, but until you forget, you're still bound to the thing and/or person who hurt you.

When I chose to not only forgive but to also forget that man who stole our money, something amazing happened. I was free! I was now free to pursue my future, unafraid and fully trusting God as I went. And what a ride it's been. But I don't think I would be here today if I hadn't forgiven *and* forgotten. Thankfully, I literally had to work to recall that incident enough to write this section. And if I sat here and thought about it, I could probably remember his name. But right now, I don't even remember.

That's freedom.

REMEMBER THE DUCK

What does bondage look like? Here's a great example:

While visiting his grandparents, little Bobby was given his first slingshot. He quickly ran and set up a practice target in the woods; however, no matter how much he trained, he never hit it. When he came back to the back yard, he spied his grandmother's pet duck. Overtaken by his impulses, the little boy pulled out his slingshot, loaded it with a rock, took aim, and let it fly. Bingo! A perfect hit. The boy panicked and, in desperation, hid the dead duck in the woodpile. There was only one problem with his strategy...

...His sister, Sally, had seen the entire thing unfold.

After lunch that day, Grandma said, "Sally, let's wash the dishes." Sally replied, "Bobby told me he wanted to help in the kitchen today. Didn't you, Bobby?" She then leaned over and whispered into his ear, "Remember the duck!" Little Bobby *gladly* did the dishes.

A bit later, Grandpa asked the children to go fishing. Grandma said, "I'm sorry, but I need Sally to help make supper." Sally smiled and said, "That's all taken care of. Bobby wants to do it." Again she whispered, "Remember the duck." Bobby stayed while Sally enjoyed an afternoon of fishing with her grandpa.

This pattern continued for several days until Bobby couldn't take it any longer. He then confessed, "Grandma, I killed your duck. I'm so sorry!" Wrapping her arms around her broken grandson she said, "I know, Bobby. I was standing at the window and saw the whole thing." "You were?" inquired Bobby. "Yes, but because I love you, I forgave you. I've been wondering how long you were going to let Sally make you a slave."

Isn't that just like the devil? He's the master of enslaving your heart and mind to things or people from your past. Maybe it was a wrong done against you, or maybe it's how you've hurt someone else. If it's the latter, then you have the power to make it right. Do it. Make it right. Then, ask forgiveness. The Bible says that God will graciously forgive you *if* you grant forgiveness to others. (See Mark 11:16.)

That's how you live a higher life.

REMEMBERING TO FORGET

Two ladies were at lunch one day when a woman walked in who had caused one much harm. Her extreme gossiping and false accusations had damaged this lady's otherwise pristine reputation. When the woman who was wronged saw her, she immediately got up from her chair and met this lady with a gracious and warm greeting. They quickly hugged, and the lady departed.

Returning to the table, the lady's friend said, "That was unbelievable! How did you do that? That woman hates you and has lied about you." She replied, "No, I don't think she has."

Her friend quickly retaliated, "How could you not remember the terrible things she's said about you?" To which the woman amazingly replied, "Because I specifically remember forgetting that!"

Again, wow.

She did more than forgive, *she remembered to forget.* And she lived a life far above "average."

THE BRICK

You might be a person who says, "Ron, you just don't understand. What happened to me was just too devastating. I can never forget it." I used to think the same way...and I lived an "average" life because of it. One more true-life example might help you get over the hump.

In 2004, Donna and I had just birthed a church in St. Petersburg, Florida. Like many new church plants, we met in a hotel. Over time, we kept noticing how one of the cleaning ladies would stop and listen to the services. (We began to wonder if she was spying on us.) One day, she asked for time off so she could sit in the service. She came and really enjoyed it. When I gave the altar call for salvation, she wanted to respond so badly but just couldn't. Donna and I knew we needed to find out why.

When we visited with her, this sweet lady told us a horrible tragedy she had recently endured. Just a few days before we began holding services in the hotel, she witnessed her husband's brutal murder at the hands of one of their close friends. She was completely consumed with unforgiveness towards this man. For the next several weeks, we ministered to her about God's love and forgiveness—specifically how God desired her to forgive this man like she had been forgiven. We also connected her to a wonderful Christian counselor friend who not only backed our efforts but took her to an entirely different level.

Our friend took this lady to the Gulf of Mexico, which is just one block away from our church, and gave her an exercise. He gave her a normal brick. Then, he told her to take all her anger, judgment, hurt, and unforgiveness and place it into that brick. He then said, "Imagine this brick is Jesus. Imagine you casting all your cares on Him and Him taking them all from you." He then showed her how God handled our sin in Micah 7:19:

> *"He will again have compassion on us, and will subdue our iniquities. You will cast all our sins into the depths of the sea."*

Now, it was time for action.

Our counselor friend had her take this brick and throw it into the sea. He then gave her an amazing instruction: "Anytime you want to hold this man's actions against him, you're going to have to dive into the ocean, find the brick, and bring it back to shore." Then, and only then, could she allow herself to fall back into her angry, unforgiving state.

One word: BREAKTHROUGH!

Oh yes, she was tempted many times to fall back into her old thought patterns, but the thought of having to recover that brick made her come to her senses. And it paid off.

Today, this sweet little hotel maid is free from the bondage that not only took her husband's life but was robbing her life as well. Not only that, she's also a powerhouse for God, telling her story everywhere and preaching God's mercy and forgiveness.

LET IT GO

So now let's talk about the person that this chapter is all about: you. Do you have wounds that are still showing? Are you constantly reopening them by replaying what happened over and over in your mind? Are you being held prisoner to your past? If so, enjoy this next barrier breaker:

 B.B.: Any area of hurt or pain that is only forgiven but not forgotten is still producing a negative harvest in your life.

It's time to uproot it and begin to live again!

No matter what you've been through (and I'm surely not making light of it), God has an incredible life waiting on the other side of your forgetfulness. Forgiving is "average;" forgetting is living the abundant life. Will you make the adjustment and live free? There's an unhindered greatness inside you just waiting to be released.

Why not stop right here and give those hurts over to God, once and for all. Pray this prayer:

"Dear Heavenly Father, I don't know if I have what it takes to forgive _____, but You said that where I'm weak, You would be strong. I couldn't save me, I had to trust You to do that supernaturally. Lord, I'm now asking You to supernaturally empower me to do what I cannot do naturally. With Your help, Father, I forgive _____ and place them into Your

hands. I choose to no longer live with the hate and the hurt. I declare, 'I am free!' Free to love and free to live to the potential You have for me! In Jesus' name. Amen."

A third, wow!

Congratulations. If you really meant what you just prayed, God is releasing you from the bondage. I know this may have been really difficult, but there's one more step that could be even harder. (I'm sure you know where I'm going with this.) Take the next step: Forget it!

Things are now shifting in the spirit realm. Understand that while forgiveness is instantaneous, restoration is a process—one that God may or may not require you to pursue. I've found true forgetfulness comes in two ways: (1.) through the restoration process or (2.) you walk away and forget it.

Wait a minute. Would God want you to just walk away? Definitely not...unless the other person refuses to become healthy enough to no longer harm you. You cannot be responsible for the actions of the other person. If they aren't doing their part in becoming healthy, then, in the words of the uber-famous Disney song, "Let it go!" When you do, you're setting your sights on a higher life.

Do you want to break the barrier of average? Then do more than forgive; forget...

...And be free.

CHAPTER 14

DO MORE THAN SHARE...GIVE

AT THE OUTSET, sharing and giving could seem to be inter-changeable terms. But, they're not. When you share, you also retain. When you give, you release. It's a huge difference. It's not wrong to share; however, it is wrong to only share what right-fully should be given.

Donna and I used to have these "conversations" concerning garage sale items. I would see something and think, *Man, we could get a lot of money for that.* Donna, on the other hand, would look at the exact same thing and say, "Hey, I wonder who we could bless with that?" "Just give it away?" I would ask. "Are you kidding me? I worked hard for that. I love that thing!" Honestly, I used to be so stinking cheap that I'd rather sell something for a dollar than give it someone I knew really needed it.

That's when I lived an "average" life.

We had a slushy maker that I loved. Oh, I forgot to mention that it had been sitting in the garage for ten years, unused! That didn't matter. I loved it. My thought was to sell it and pocket the three dollars it would bring. Donna? She had a different view. "Ron, you know that John's been out of work. I bet his three kids would love this slushy machine, especially since it's been ninety-five degrees for the last three weeks." I felt like Adam in the book of Genesis: "God, this woman you gave me!" Here she was, yielding to the devil in the stewarding decision. I reasoned with God, "God, we're talking about thirty cents of tithe here! You said it yourself, 'He who is faithful in the little things...'"

In a moment of divine inspiration, I grabbed the slushy maker, ran about twenty steps, then turned and defiantly looked at Donna. How dare she mess with the priest of our home! Of course, she just rolled her eyes and said, "Whatever!" as she walked away. Only the Lord and I understand how close she came to compromising our entire life of stewardship that day.

It wasn't long after this when God spoke a divinely prophetic word into my life: "Ron, you're cheap!" For months I was sure He meant, "frugal." It was probably a bad translation from the Greek or something. But over time I came to accept the fact: I really was cheap. Then I did an about face. It was time to make up for lost time.

With my new revelation, I started cleaning house. When I found something we didn't need or use, I'd think of someone who could use it and drove it to them. If I didn't know anyone, I ran the item down to the end of our driveway and stuck a "Free" sign on it. Wow, what a great feeling...until one "morning after."

Donna woke up one day and went to the kitchen to make some toast. Then she asked, "Ron, where's the toaster?" I proudly told her, "Donna, some blessed person is enjoying toast this morning." She then went to make some eggs...and asked, "Ron, where's the frying pan?"

You get the picture.

I finally got the pendulum of giving to the center, but it was difficult.

THE BEST OF THE BEST

In all that process, here's what I learned about myself: I like stuff! And, if I'm going to let my stuff go, I want something in return. Stingy, cheap, and selfish were the three attributes I had easily mastered. But the three that really mattered—sowing, generosity, and blessing others—took some work. It's not just me. We all have a selfish nature. The "old" man doesn't die easily, but to live a life far above "average," there must be a funeral.

Today, Donna and I have a deal. Neither of us will make a purchase over $100 without the other's consent. We also don't sow anything over $100 in value without being in agreement. The results? Over the years we've given away furniture, clothes, cars, two houses (free and clear), and close to a half million dollars in cash. I'm not bragging on us; I'm bragging on Him! Oh, and guess what? God keeps supplying more seed for us to sow. We're like a Kingdom brokerage house.

I call that busting through the barrier of "average" in a big way.

The best giver to ever exist was God. He's done a pretty amazing job modeling this giving thing. Romans 8:32 explains:

> *"He who did not spare His own Son, but delivered Him up for us all, how shall He not with Him also freely give us all things?"*

Can you imagine? We squirm when God asks us to give one thousand dollars, or a piece of furniture, or a car, when He gave His only Son to die for us. John 3:16 reminds us that because God loved, He gave. But, it doesn't stop there. Now we are required to pay it forward. Jesus said:

> *"...For everyone to whom much is given, from him much will be required..."*

Luke 12:48

In other words, we're required to give too.
Not convinced yet? How about this:

> *"But this I say: He who sows sparingly will also reap sparingly, and he who sows bountifully will also reap bountifully. So let each one give as he purposes in his heart, not grudgingly or of necessity; for God loves a cheerful giver."*

2 Corinthians 9:6-7

Over time, I went from an un-cheerful hoarder to a hilarious giver. Which one sounds "average" to you? That's an easy answer. Here's the good news: You, like me, can destroy "average" in this arena. Do you want to break that barrier? Then do more than share...

...Give.

(Oh, do you know anyone looking for a slushy machine? I have one for $3.00!)

CHAPTER 15

DO MORE THAN DECIDE...DISCERN

ONE OF MY mentors, Bishop Tony Miller, was on a flight and happened to sit next to a well-known denominational pastor. In conversation, he asked this pastor, "What do you feel is the biggest need in the American church today?" Without hesitation, the pastor replied, "Discernment."

Let's take that a step further: What's the biggest need in people today? I believe the answer's the same: discernment—the ability to see beyond the obvious.

A few years ago, I was in Israel with a group from our church. Among them was my very special friend, David. David is blind. Let me rephrase that: David is unsighted. There's a big difference.

When we visited the Garden Tomb, we couldn't go very far. There were bars—kind of like jail house bars—constructed to keep the public from the rocks where Jesus' body would have been laid. I felt bad that David couldn't experience this, so I asked the curator to let him behind the bars. He consented, with the condition that no one else from our group accompany him. It was just David, the curator, and myself.

The experience in itself was amazing, but David made it even better. While feeling all around the tomb, he stayed quiet. That was until he reached the last foot of the table where Jesus was laid. At that point, David began to weep. I dared not interrupt. After about a half hour, David composed himself enough to share what had just taken place.

He said "The artisan who chiseled out the tomb (it's literally cut out of a rock wall) had done a very uniform job. Then, about six inches from the end, the chiseling definitely changed. It was much rougher...obviously done in haste." His account perfectly coincides with John 19:38-42. There, the Bible says that this tomb, which belonged to Joseph of Arimathea, was a "new" tomb—one where no one had ever laid. Some extra biblical writings tell us that Joseph was small in stature. David discerned what we couldn't: that the tomb had been hurriedly made a bit larger.

That reality rocked his world.

The decision to get behind the bars and into the tomb allowed David's discernment to be exponentially increased. And what he discerned made God's Word come even more alive to him.

To live above "average," you must learn to discern. Let me rephrase that: you must *yearn* to discern!

HOW DO YOU KNOW?

Discernment isn't only a requirement to live an abundant life, it's also something God condones. One of the first instructions God gave His people, through the Levitical priest, was to teach discernment.

Gog and his armies had taken Israel captive, but God destroyed Gog and all his troops. It took Israel seven months to bury the dead. God's first directive was, "Have a feast to celebrate." After the feast, the next instruction was for Israel to build a temple of worship. Then, the Lord gave the priests His expectations for them. These were His instructions:

> *"And they shall teach My people the difference between the holy and the unholy, and cause them to discern between the unclean and the clean."*

—Ezekiel 44:23

Since discernment is so important to God, then wouldn't it be a good thing to understand it a bit more? While there are many definitions, I see discernment as an intentional process of opening to God's will, utilizing reason, faith, and prayerful reflection so that our choices are aligned more closely with God's purposes.

B.B.: Discernment flourishes in a context of regular spiritual practices, along with a suspension of personal agendas.

Solomon, the wisest man who ever lived, encourages us on the value of discernment:

"My son, if you receive my words, and treasure my commands within you, so that you incline your ear to wisdom, and apply your heart to understanding; yes, if you cry out for discernment, and lift up your voice for understanding, if you seek her as silver, and search for her as for hidden treasures; then you will understand the fear of the Lord, and find the knowledge of God."

Proverbs 2:1-5

Discernment is a small word that can make a huge difference in your life. How do you know if you have it? Here are few clues. Discernment is:

- the ability to tell good from bad, even when the facts are void, vague, or deceptive.
- the navigational tool of life.
- the ability to follow God in a mixed up world.
- the ability to know more than you know.
- the illumination of darkness.
- the power to build dependency on God and less on yourself.
- the ability to judge motives and know methods.

THAT MAN IN THE STATION

On a cold January morning, a man took his violin into a Washington, D.C., metro station during the morning rush hour. As he sat, he began playing—not just any music, but six Bach pieces. For about forty-five minutes, he played. At that time of the morning, thousands of people must have passed by, hustling to their jobs, yet only a few discerned what was truly happening.

After about three minutes, a middle-aged man noticed this man was playing. He slowed his pace, stopped for a few seconds, and then hurried to meet his schedule. About a minute later, the violinist received his first tip—change thrown into the till by a woman who never stopped to listen. Not long after, another man leaned against the wall to listen, but quickly looked at his watch and moved on.

Of all the thousands who passed by that morning, only one three-year-old boy really stopped to listen. Tagging behind his hurried mother, the boy halted his mom, but only for a few minutes. As they scurried down the station, the boy never took his eyes off the violinist as he continued to play. Several children followed suit.

At morning's end, the station was cleared. No applause, no recognition. Only a tip jar which contained a mere thirty-two dollars, mostly in loose pocket change. What people failed to realize that morning was the greatness which was in their very midst.

You see, the violinist was Joshua Bell, one of the best musicians in the world. That day, he played a violin valued at over three million dollars. Two days before this experiment, Joshua Bell sold out a Boston concert hall, with ticket prices well into the hundreds of dollars each.

No one discerned greatness that day. It makes me wonder, *What do we walk by, every day, and fail to discern?* Valuable people. Great opportunities. God's priceless vessels. "Average" people never discern these things.

Above average people do.

DON'T LEAVE HOME WITHOUT IT

Discernment is one of the most invaluable tools to destroy the enemy called "average." It has saved me much trouble over the years—maybe even saved my life on a few occasions.

After the devastating earthquake that rocked the nation of Haiti in 2010, our church raised enough funds to rebuild a Christian school in Leogane, the quake's epicenter. We shipped the materials from Miami, Florida, and then a small group from the church with building experience headed down for a Saturday to Saturday trip.

When we landed in Port a Prince, discernment kicked in. Inside my spirit man I heard, "Change your ticket." I shrugged it off. Then, an even more pronounced warning: "Change your ticket to Thursday." I told the men traveling with me what I heard. Their consensus was, "It's just nerves." I asked them to make it a point of prayer overnight. The next day, their opinion changed. They all agreed that I heard correctly. Discernment had won, so I jumped into action.

I called Donna right away and said, "Honey, will you find out what it cost to change our tickets?" She did the research and found it to be $150 per person. "No way!" I said. (Remember I told you I was cheap.) Then she said, "Ron, there's a tropical storm brewing in the Atlantic, but it's not supposed to come near Haiti." While she was talking, I heard once again, "Change your tickets!" That was it. Even though my frugal self was screaming, "NO!" I told her to change the tickets. She did, and we booked the last available seats…

…On the last available flight before Category 2 hurricane Tomas hit Haiti.

Actually, it wasn't the last flight back to the U.S. The last evacuation flight, which left right behind us, crashed in Cuba. There were no survivors.

Just like in the Apostle Paul's journeys, the Holy Spirit constrained and compelled us to make a change. Discernment, along with (somewhat delayed) obedience, literally saved our lives. From that time on, I have treated discernment like my American Express card...

...I don't leave home without it!

HOW WE SEE

Discernment is a lifestyle for those who live far above the status quo. How does discernment come? The primary way is through prayer.

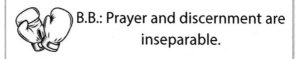

B.B.: Prayer and discernment are inseparable.

You can't have one without the other. Authentic prayer opens your heart and mind to God's presence and purposes. That's where discernment is found.

The second most powerful way to grow in discernment is by reading God's Word, every day. Hebrews 4:12 says:

> *"For the word of God is living and powerful, and sharper than any two-edged sword, piercing even to the division of soul and spirit, and of joints and marrow, and is a discerner of the thoughts and intents of the heart."*

Daily prayer and a steady digestion of the Bible will acquaint you with your Heavenly Father's voice. Contrary to what some theologians say, God still speaks to His children today! Hearing His voice allows you to engage your intellect and reason. Although prayer and Bible reading are the primary conditions for discernment, utilizing your understanding and action is also employed in the process.

Everyone views the world through a different set of lenses. We categorize information and experiences through many filters. We don't really see things how they are; we see them how *we* are! Discernment is the tool that moves us past what we see from our world into the realm that God sees.

Discernment is powerful. Someone once asked the New York Philharmonic Orchestra to name their most effective conductor. Arturo Toscanini won hands down. When asked why, one instrumentalist said, "He could anticipate when you were about to make a mistake and keep you from making it."

That's the power of discernment.

What are you seeing right now? Are you only looking at the world through spiritual cataracts on your own eyes? What opportunities are you missing? What dangers loom that you need to be forewarned of? Discernment is the key. Learn to hear its voice. Obey quickly and watch what happens. It could save your life.

Do you want to break the barrier of average? Then do more than make decisions…

…Yearn to discern.

CHAPTER 16

DO MORE THAN
"BAHA"...NAVIGATE

BEFORE JUMPING INTO this chapter, let's go back to the very first one. Remember my comment after the story about the boy who drowned? I said, "As I lay here on the beach of life, short of breath but alive, I want to scream, 'Why didn't anybody teach me to swim?'" This chapter probably makes me want to scream the loudest!

But first, something quite humorous.

I read a story online about a very un-average lady. It went something like this:

> *The other day I went to the Christian book store and saw a "Honk if You Love Jesus" bumper sticker. I was feeling particularly sassy that day, because I had just come from a thrilling choir performance, followed by a thunderous prayer meeting. So, I bought the sticker and*

put it on my bumper. Boy, am I glad I did! What an uplifting experience that followed.

I was at a red light, at a busy intersection, lost in thought about the Lord and how good He is, and I didn't notice that the light had changed. It is a good thing that someone else loves Jesus because if he hadn't honked, I would never have noticed!

I found lots of people love Jesus. Why? Well, while I was sitting there, the guy behind me started honking like crazy, and then he got so excited, he leaned out his window and screamed "For the love of God! Go! Go!" My bumper sticker must have got him thinking about how good Jesus is. He was so excited, he just kept screaming His name over and over. What an exuberant cheerleader that man was for Jesus!

I just leaned out my window and started waving to all these loving people. I even honked my horn a few times to share in the love!

I saw another guy waving in a funny way with only his middle finger sticking up in the air. When I asked my teenage grandson in the backseat what it meant, he said it was probably a Hawaiian "good luck" sign. Well, I've never been to Hawaii, so I leaned out the window and gave him the good luck sign back. My grandson burst out laughing. Even he was enjoying this experience!

A few more people got so caught up in the joy of the moment that they got out of their cars and started walking towards me. I bet they wanted to pray, or ask what church I attended, being that my love for Jesus had started this revival. But this is when I noticed the light had changed. So, I waved to all my sisters and brothers, smiling really big at them, because I was just so happy. I then drove through the intersection.

I noticed I was the only car that got through the intersection before the light changed again, and I felt kind of sad that I had to leave them after all the love we had shared. So I slowed the car down, leaned out the window and gave them all the Hawaiian good luck sign one last time as I drove away.

Praise the Lord for such wonderful folks! GTG for now,

Love,

Ethel

We laugh at such a clueless scenario, but the truth is less laughable and equally "clueless" situations happen all the time. And with much greater trauma, drama, and harm.

LET'S GO BAHA-ING

Think with me for a second. How much money do you spend on your car each month just to keep it rolling? I'm talking about gas, tires, oil changes, repairs, etc. Three hundred dollars? Five hundred? Yet when it comes life's most important vehicles, we spend—or should I say, invest—almost nothing. What vehicles am I referring to? Our most precious gift on the planet: people.

"Ron, how are people a vehicle?" I'm glad you asked.

People are God's vehicles in the earth. They're what He chooses to move us to destinations like increase, advancement, assignment, happiness, purpose, and joy. All of these places, and more, are delivered through people. So, how do we invest in this vehicle? Let me show you.

But first, let me tell you a true story—one which I will reference again later.

When I was around fifteen years old, I loved hanging around my older brother and his friends. They always did much cooler stuff than me and my friends. (Okay, maybe it was *stupider* stuff.) One thing they did was called "Baha-ing." Here's what this word means.

Our house was surrounded by hundreds of acres of fields. When we Baha-ed, we took one of our, or our friend's, vehicles and tore through the fields as fast as we could. Sometimes, the fields had been freshly planted. Other times, young plants were starting to sprout. Wherever we went, we left a path of destruction and a great deal of damage in our wake. But we didn't care. Having a good time was far more important.

Now hold that thought. We'll come back here a bit later.

THE HIDDEN TREASURE

Back to investing in people. How does that happen exactly? We've become experts in investing our money, mainly because there are so many vehicles and tools to help. Counselors, brokers, bankers, software, seminars, apps, analysts, television shows, and so on. We cling to these like glue mainly because most of us can't afford to lose any of our precious money. So, we go to great lengths to find the latest and greatest information to help us hang on to it for dear life.

Not so when it comes to people.

Sadly, there's very little training and only a few tools

available to help us develop and maintain the vehicle called people. Consequently, whether we are clueless like Ethel and her Hawaiian good luck sign or purposely and callously malicious like me and my brother's friends' Baha experiences, people live with much hurt, confusion, anger, and brokenness. But, here's the good news: There is help!

There are tools to be used.

Over the years, I've discovered some amazing resources which have helped me become the best possible version of "me." They've also helped countless other people, too. It's powerful and accurate information that has allowed me to make good investments into the people around me, with the highest yield of increase. Now, instead of Baha-ing callously through other people's fields, I can navigate in such a way that it doesn't leave a destructive wake but actually uncovers great treasure.

I'm a pretty protective person by nature. Whenever I'm on our Ohio farm and I see some pick-up truck passing through the gate onto our property, my heart rate goes up. But if it's the gas company coming to maintain our well, that's a different story. Yes, they're driving across our field, but it's to help protect our treasure and investments.

People are like this, too. We all have hidden treasures. But how can we find it? Jesus gave us the answer:

> *"Again, the kingdom of heaven is like treasure hidden in a field, which a man found and hid; and for joy over it he goes and sells all that he has and buys that field."*

> Matthew 13:44

Treasure is hidden in fields. What's a field? It's a bunch of dirt. The value lies in someone's ability to move it. Our gas reserves lay under dirt. Gold is excavated from underground. Diamonds are mined from far beneath the soil. You usually have to move a lot of dirt to get to the treasure. I'm so thankful for the people in my life who saw beyond all my "dirt" on the surface and dug out the treasure. It makes me think:

 B.B.: "Average" people only see dirt. People who live far above average chose to be treasure hunters.

Anybody can recklessly Baha through other people's lives, but the Kingdom of Heaven is looking for treasure hunters! When you navigate onto someone else's fields (aka their life) with the purpose of discovering treasure, you have some dirt to move. It's okay to get dirty. Keep it up, and you will develop into a valued treasure hunter.

START DIGGING

Who moved your dirt to discover the hidden treasure in you? How about communicating some thankfulness to them? Go ahead. Put down this book and do it now. Facebook them, call them, text them. Whatever method you use, do it now. Thankfulness is a pay day for treasure hunters. Not only will you blow them away, you'll motivate them to continue excavating in you and others. And by doing so, you'll be maintaining their treasure.

Everybody wins.

Let's take it a step further. What fields has God assigned you to uncover? Are you doing it? Are you Baha-ing over everything in your path or skillfully and purposefully navigating through someone's dirt to excavate the treasure? "Well, Ron, that sounds good, but just how do I do it?" Again, thank you for asking.

The number one way to become a valued and trusted treasure hunter is through questions. That's right. Questions. They are the shovels which penetrate someone's surface dirt.

 B.B.: It's impossible to be on a quest without asking quest-ions.

Questions provide the greatest access to others self-discovery. They're also your greatest access to the someone else's wisdom. Quality questions provide the building blocks for a quality life. Proverbs 20:5 says:

> *"The purpose in a man's heart is like deep water,*
> *but a man of understanding will draw it out."*

(ESV)

Questions are the bucket that draws out purpose from other people's wells. They not only work to discover purpose in others, they also work to discover purpose *in you*.

One day, my pastor, myself, and three other men were leaving Ethiopia on our way back home. We had just finished conducting evangelistic crusades where hundreds of thousands came to Christ. It was about a six-hour drive back to Addis Ababa. One young man who was with us—a very energetic green-horn—began asking my pastor some questions. Things like:

- "What's the best book you ever read?"
- "In the ministry, what's the toughest spot you've ever been in, and how did you get out of it?"
- "How do you prepare to teach?"
- "What makes you laugh?"
- "What makes you cry?"

On and on he went. He just wouldn't shut up! He made me so mad, and I was so frustrated—but not like you may think.

Do you know what ticked me off the most? It wasn't this young man constantly running his mouth. Rather, it was the fact that he unearthed more treasure from my pastor's heart in a few hours than I had in fourteen years. How?

Questions.

One of my closest friends, Dennis McIntee, is a question-asking master. He's better than anyone I've ever known. Even though he came from a very difficult background, Dennis now sits in some of the highest level board rooms in America, counseling and coaching their top executives and leaders. He's also equally respected in many European nations. How did he get there? With formal education? No. Did he have the wealth to buy his way into these circles? Certainly not. Was it a few big breaks? Nope. He arrived at these positions one way: by asking brilliant questions.

And he lives an exceptional life, one far beyond the realm of "average."

WHAT'S THE PROBLEM?

There are a few reasons why people don't ask many questions. One is because they don't like navigating the answers. Another reason is they just don't want to spend the time to dig past the surface soil and into the real, underlying issues. Most counselors say that during a conversation, you have to ask, "What's the problem" about seven times to unveil the real issue. Here's a great example:

Hey, Bill, how are you?

Oh, man. Rough day.

Oh, really? What seems to be the problem?

Well, my kids heard Gina and I arguing last night.

Sorry to hear that. What's the problem?

I don't know. Maybe I was just impatient with her, but I really lost my temper.

That's not good. What's the problem with you and Gina?

You know, ever since last night, I've been wondering about that.

And?

Well, it makes me so mad when she always has to know my whereabouts. Dang, I can't be somewhere for thirty minutes without getting blasted with, "Where have you been?"

So, why's that a problem?

I don't know. I guess it goes back to when I cheated on her.

Oh, so you think the real problem is trust?

Yeah, I guess so. She just doesn't trust me anymore.

What can you do about that?

I guess I could probably be more diligent in letting her know where I am. But man, I just feel like I'm on trial or something.

Well, is your wife's trust and the happiness of your kids worth it?

You sure ask hard questions! Yes, it's definitely worth it.

So, when will you start?

Right now. I'll call her and tell her I'm with you!

How many "average" people would bypass this conversation simply because they don't want to hear the answers? Their conversation wouldn't have gotten past the third line. "Just not myself today." "Oh man, bummer. Hope the rest of your day is better." Boom. Done. Out of here. See ya! Easy peasy! That's what is called Baha-ing.

And "average" people do it every single day.

WHAT DO YOU SEEK?

I can already hear you saying, "Ron, this sounds good and all, but I don't want to be a busy body, sticking my nose where it doesn't belong." I wholeheartedly agree with you. And if you're prying just to hear—or worse yet, to gossip—then please don't bother. Stay "average."

The truth is, people are looking for real love. Non-condemning, non-combative, real "from the heart" love. Nobody likes a know-it-all. That's why learning the art of questioning is so crucial. Asking the right non-invasive questions which lead someone down the path of self-discovery is the way to unbury what lies beneath.

Friend, you are God's great treasure hunter! Transformed people transform people. You are God's transformer. Anybody can see the dirt, but God has given you the ability to see the treasure. It all comes down to what you're looking for in people.

Two kinds of birds fly over a desert: buzzards and hummingbirds. Buzzards find dead, stinking carcasses for food while hummingbirds look for a cactus flower. Both are hungry. Both have the same need. It comes down to what they seek. It's the same for you: You find what you seek. Are you looking for the dirt in others? You'll sure find it. I can guarantee it! But if you search for the gold, you'll surely find it, too.

What are you seeking?

 B.B.: You will always see the realm that's most prevalent in your own life.

If you always see the dirt in others, it's probably because it's all you see in your own life. Ask God to grant you the incredible gift to see beyond the surface. Find the good...no, find the *great* in yourself and in others. It's there; it just needs to be unearthed.

Ask questions. Dig and dig with the intention of helping

move yourself, and others, from "average" to amazing. Do you want to defeat the enemy called average? Then throw out the dune buggy. Do more than Baha...

...Navigate.

CHAPTER 17

DO MORE THAN THINK...PLAN

HERE'S AN INTERESTING statistic: If you're thinking about where you're going in life and the resources/vehicles it will take to get you there, you're in the top twenty-five percent of society. However, if you have a written plan on how to accomplish your dreams, that puts you in the top four percent of Americans! That's right, only four percent of people have taken the time to clearly define their objectives *and* have a written a plan of action.

They are also the ones who kick "average" in the teeth.

Can you imagine what a house would look like if it were built without a set of plans? An architect's drawing focuses much more on the building's form and function rather than just meeting codes. Everything they plan is strategically placed to work in conjunction and harmony with everything else. The plans are the key.

Many other areas in life entirely function around plans. Take a surgical procedure for example. Would you go into an operation with a doctor who said, "You know, I don't quite know how all this works nor how I'm going to go about this, but let's get started shall we?" No, you wouldn't. Think about how much planning goes into the football game you watch on televison, a movie you enjoy at the theatre, or the roads you drive on every day. What would a car look like if the auto plant had no plans to follow? Scary!

Plans are everywhere, yet most people stumble through life without any life-plan whatsoever. Maybe that's why over ninety-five percent of people who hit retirement aren't happy with where they are in life. Ninety-six percent live with no written plan; ninety-five percent end up at the wrong place. Do you see a pattern here?

What in the world is wrong with us?

Let's talk about making a daily plan. If you're like me, you probably find yourself spending more time putting out fires on the days you don't plan ahead. It's the price of being unprepared for the day. You see, a plan makes you proactive—and they are easy to formulate.

Start by thinking about what you want to do that day and how you're going to do. That's the first step, but don't stop there. If you don't take the next step and *write down your plan*, all your wholesome, efficient, strategic thoughts may never come forth. It's easy: Make a plan. Write it down. Then work your plan.

You might argue, "Well, Ron, I can't plan out my day. There are too many variables. Things change too quickly. Besides, many things depend on other people." Blah, blah, blah, blah. Do you think you're so unique? Do you really think that no one else has similar issues? Heck, almost everyone I know could say the exact same thing. Here's the difference: "Average" people complain about making a plan. Those who live on a higher plane do something about it—and succeed in life.

B.B.: Plan your work then work your plan.

ONE THING

In the early 1900's, U.S. Steel hired a consulting firm and gave them a specific assignment. For six months, the firm was to review the entire nationwide operation—from ore extraction to production, to sales and management. They were then to present just one idea which would have the greatest impact to increase productivity.

For the next six months, forty executives spent countless hours studying the business. They traveled to every mine, plant, and office, interviewing blue and white collar workers alike. At the end of the tenure, the top consulting executives were flown to the company's headquarters to reveal their one revolutionary idea.

The presentation was so heavy that the president of the consulting firm presented it himself. After the enormous conference room was silenced, the U.S. Steel CEO introduced the firm's president, which in turn addressed the CEO, "Sir, before you sit down, would you mind writing down your plans for today?" The CEO responded, "Right now?" "Yes," replied the president. Complying with the request, he then took out a sheet of paper and wrote down his plan for the day.

After handing in his plan, the CEO asked, "Can we now

get on with your recommendations? We're all anxious to hear your one idea." Then the presenter said, "Actually, I'm finished." "What?" exclaimed the company's leader. "You haven't told us anything!" The president responded, "Actually, sir, I have. The paper I hold in my hand contains our one idea. If all your management team would do this same exercise every day, it would revolutionize your entire organization."

The CEO screamed, "Get out!" He also swore that the consulting firm would never see a penny for such a sham. And with that, the company's boss retreated to his office in such a foul mood he could hardly think.

After a few moments, he began to think, *What was I supposed to do today?* Then, he remembered his daily action plan. Being an intelligent man, he reasoned, *Well, at least something positive came out of this six months. Maybe it wasn't all wasted time.* So, the CEO worked off his daily plan and soon came to a stark realization: Even though he was distracted by the morning's atrocity, he was more productive that day than he had been in a long time.

Was it a fluke? Maybe. To further test the waters, the CEO wrote out a plan for the next day, then the next, then the next. After thirty days, he ordered his immediate staff to do the same. Efficiency and productivity suddenly shot through the roof. He eventually required the entire company to write daily plans. After one year, U.S. Steel was more lucrative than ever. To honor his commitment, the CEO sent an apology letter to the consulting firm, along with a check for four times the original contract agreement!

Writing the plan is the "one thing."

TAKE THE CHALLENGE

What benefited U.S. Steel many years ago is still working today. So, let me give you this very same assignment—a challenge if you will.

Take out a sheet of paper. You heard me right, a sheet of paper! I know your laptop, iPad, smart phone, and other gadgets have a "to do" feature, but until you separate it, learn it, and appreciate it, you'll never do it electronically. It's not important to you yet. So...

...Take out a sheet of paper. At the top of the page, put the word "task." Drop down a quarter of the page and write "phone calls." Halfway down, write "meetings." At the three-quarter mark, put "errands." Now it's time to make your plan.

Under each heading, list the tasks, phone calls, meetings, and errands you need to do tomorrow. Now put a small box in front of each item. That's it. Easy.

Tomorrow, start working off your list. When you accomplish an item, fill in the box. If you don't finish it, fill it halfway. (e.g., maybe you left a message on one phone call.) If you don't get to an item, leave the box blank.

The next day, make a new list starting with the things unfinished from the previous day. List those items first, then write new items. Now, make a file (yes, an old-school file!) and label whatever month you're in. Place all lists from that month into the file. BAM! Now you have a permanent record to reference if needed. It's very easy to convert this to electronic planning, but do it on paper until you get it down.

I can promise you, using this simple planning tool will revolutionize your entire life. As simple as it seems, it's the most powerful way to increase your daily productivity. So, when do you start? Consider the words of General George S. Patton: "A good plan today is better than a perfect plan tomorrow." Start today!

 B.B.: If you fail to plan, you plan to fail.

You better believe it. Come on. Step out of the ordinary life. Put yourself into the top four percent in America. Write your plan—daily, weekly, monthly, yearly, and long term. You can do it. Kick down that barrier of average by not only thinking…

…Start planning.

CHAPTER 18

DO MORE THAN TRY...PERSEVERE

AT SIX THOUSAND feet in the air, I was all alone and hopelessly lost. To make matters worse, my little Cessna 170 was out of fuel. After six months of pilot training, I had just received my solo check off, which meant I could now fly without an instructor. It started out as one of the happiest days of my life.

One requirement to receive a full pilot's license is to complete a cross-country solo flight. That simply means you must fly alone for at least one hundred and fifty nautical miles and land at three different airports. This was my maiden voyage. It was time to do this "big time!"

My first leg was to fly from Kent State University in Kent, Ohio, to Ashtabula, Ohio. My flight plan was filed, the plane was checked out and ready to go, and I took off. Practically every VFR flight journey has what's called "way points" along the route. These are set in place to make sure you are tracking correctly to your destination. The only problem was that on my route, there was nothing but corn fields and cow pastures. I couldn't find anything that even resembled a way point.

Not good.

Being from that area, I had a pretty good idea how long my flight should take. The time came when I should've arrived at my destination, but there wasn't an airport in sight. Only a few little tiny towns were in view. So, I continued flying, hoping I would see the airport shortly. All the while, my gas gauges continued to slip towards "E." Something wasn't right.

I decided to buzz the next town to see if I could recognize my location. I probably came in way too low and scared the good folks in this sleepy little town to death, but I was desperate.

My first shot was to look at the water tower. Surely, there would be a city name proudly painted on it. So, I buzzed the tower. Nothing! I then figured that the next rational step would be to fly tree top height and look for a "Welcome to…" sign. Again, nothing. I repeated this same routine at two more towns, both with the same results. It was obvious that these folks didn't want anyone to know who they were…

…Especially wayward student pilots.

By now I was dangerously low on fuel. It was time to declare an emergency. I climbed back up to six thousand feet and called the air traffic control tower I was assigned to in Cleveland, Ohio. I told them I was a student pilot and that I was lost. There was only one problem: *They couldn't find me on their radar.* Their explanation was that a weather system had come through and the winds might have blown me further east. So, they turned me over to the Youngstown, Ohio, control. Problem number two: *They couldn't find me either.* Oh my gosh! As the plane was literally running on fumes, I begin rifling through the emergency kit looking for a box of Depends!

Youngstown turned me over to Erie, Pennsylvania. Thank the Lord, they found me, but I was in a completely different state.

I relay this story not to brag about my exceptional pilot skills as a youth (yeah, right), but to make a point tied to this chapter. On that flight, I did more than try; I persevered! Trust me, crashing that plane wasn't an option for me. I was going to find a way—someway, somehow—to land it. There was no way I was going to become part of the local landscape that day.

Thank God, perseverance won.

PPP/OPP

In my life experiences, I've come to see the power of perseverance pay big dividends in two separate arenas. There's what I call PPP which means, "Personal Profit Perseverance," and there's OPP, "Other's Profit Perseverance." These two are in the same boat as lust vs. love. PPP, much like lust, is a self-benefit at someone else's expense. OPP, on the other hand, mimics true love: benefiting others at the expense of self.

Anyone can do PPP, which benefits themselves. Only those with a heart after Jesus will live an OPP life.

When you begin looking at life through the OPP lens, you become empowered on an entirely different level. It's easy to accomplish greatness when you are the lone benefactor. But what about living an extraordinary, beyond average life for the benefit of others? Isn't it time to start looking beyond PPP and start accomplishing great things for those around you? "Average" people live for PPP. Truly great people are OPP driven.

Do you remember Richard Rescorla? He's an OPP person.

While you probably don't remember his name, you surely are familiar with his great accomplishments.

Richard Rescorla was instrumental in evacuating thousands of people during the 9/11 attacks. As the security director for Morgan Stanley, Rescorla was a stickler for the south tower's occupants' safety. Twice a year, he held emergency evacuation drills to train people in case they needed to flee the building. His training paid off.

On the morning of September 11, 2001, the World Trade Center's north tower was struck. Rescorla put his plan into action. He calmly reminded people of their training and even assisted them out of the building. With pandemonium, sheer chaos, and terror all around, Rescorla helped to successfully evacuate over twenty-five hundred people. He persevered right up until the moment the south tower was struck—and he was killed.

But, because he was an OPP person, thousands lived.

LIVE THE LIFE

Jesus talked about this kind of OPP sacrifice in John 15:13 when He said:

> *"Greater love has no one than this, than to lay down one's life for his friends."*

I'm not advocating that you have to die to fulfill this scripture. But if you don't start doing this in the little things of life, you'll *never* do it with your whole life. Again, OPP is simply sacrificing for others, often at the expense of self. And it pays HUGE dividends—both in this life and the life to come.

One of the best examples of this was Mother Theresa. Here

was a lady who possessed practically nothing except an OPP heart, yet she not only helped thousands, she became world famous—and Heaven famous, too.

Just think what would have happened if Richard Rescorla was an "average" PPP person? He probably would have told those people, "Well, I tried. I hope you remember what I taught you. I'm outta' here!"

Thankfully, he persevered until the end.

While PPP screams, "Get!", OPP says, "Give!" Aren't these the two basic categories everyone on the planet falls under? Takers or givers? PPP or OPP? "Average" or super-empowered awesome life? Which one do you choose?

The Apostle Paul said it this way:

> *"Let nothing be done through selfish ambition or conceit, but in lowliness of mind let each esteem others better than himself. Let each of you look out not only for his own interests, but also for the interests of others."*

Philippians 2:3-4

Man, if that isn't OPP, I don't know what is!

One other thing. You can live an "average" PPP life and struggle, or you can choose the OPP route which *automatically attracts the grace of God.* Oh, yes it does.

> *"But He gives more grace. Therefore He says: 'God resists the proud, but gives grace to the humble.'"*

James 4:6

To get an "A" on God's report card (which, by the way, stands for "awesome life"), you'll have to do more than try. You must persevere!

JUST DO

Perseverance isn't as difficult as it may seem. Sometimes, it just means showing up…and sticking with it. William Wilberforce, an eighteenth-century English politician who was instrumental in stopping the slave trade, once said: "Our motto must continue to be perseverance. And ultimately I trust the Almighty will crown our efforts with such." His thoughts perfectly concur with the Bible:

> *"For you have need of endurance, so that after you have done the will of God, you may receive the promise."*
>
> Hebrews 10:36

> *"…but we also glory in tribulations, knowing that tribulation produces perseverance; and perseverance, character; and character, hope. Now hope does not disappoint, because the love of God has been poured out in our hearts by the Holy Spirit who was given to us."*
>
> Romans 5:3-5

In the Star Wars movie, *The Empire Strikes Back*, Yoda instructs Luke Skywalker to use the Force to help him retrieve his spaceship out of a bog where it has sunk using only his mind. Luke obviously thinks this is impossible. After encouragement from Yoda, Luke reluctantly agrees to "give it a try." Then, the great "prophet" Yoda spoke his infamous words: "No. Try not. Do. Or do not. There is no try."

Just think where you might be today if you listened to Yoda. What if you upheld his standard of "There is no try!"? It's not like you don't have the ability. Paul wrote in Philippians 4:13 that you can do all things through Christ who gives you the strength. How many things? All. The last time I checked, "all" meant all!

MOVING ON

Looking back over your life, can you see a trail of things you've tried and left undone? I'm sure you can. We all have them. That's when you lived an "average" life. But, that's changing. "Trying" is changing to persevering—sticking with something until it's completed.

There are probably some things you need to just leave in the past, too. You know, the things that didn't work out then and probably won't work now, either. I love the saying, "If your horse is dead, dismount!" Leave them be, and move on.

Your enemy would love for you to camp in the valley of defeat, staring at its landscape. The truth is, you can do very little about things lost due to a lack of perseverance. But, you *can* decide, here and now, that you won't be robbed of your future. There's nothing as powerful as a made up mind.

Perseverance is never easy. Remember Galatians 6:9 that says to not grow weary, for in due season you will reap if you don't lose heart.

 B.B.: When you lose heart, persevering gives way to trying.

Don't let it! You're doing good. You're on your way to reaping.

Here's one more challenge: Grab another piece of paper and write two columns: "try" and "persevere." Under "try", write down the things you're tempted to give up on but, with the Holy Spirit's help, you're committing to persevere in. One by one, move them to the "persevere" side. Do you see it? Now, watch what happens. You can, *and will*, do all things.

It's time to say, "Bye-bye average," and "Hello awesome!" To do that, stop trying…

…Start preserving.

CHAPTER 19

DO MORE THAN DREAM...DO

DREAMS AND VISIONS are God's blueprints to shape your life. Your heart is the incubator for God's dream, but that's just the beginning. People who live average lives stop there. Once a dream is birthed, it takes your life, heart, and resources to do the dream. That's where the harvest is found.

Have I told you that Donna and I love to camp? Just wanted to make sure you knew! Anyways, when we are trying to find a new camping place, we use a roadmap or our GPS. It's a great tool to help navigate us to known places. However, once we start hiking, the GPS is useless. There are no roads, no turn offs, no exits, nothing. Just woods, fields, and trails not shown on any navigational system. That's when we pull out the old trusted compass to help guide us to our destination.

The same is true for your life.

Right now, you may be cruising along fine with just a map. But in order to fulfill all the possibilities God has placed inside you, you will need a compass. A roadmap isn't going to cut it. It's called trading in your comfort for the risk of the unknown. You see, God's looking for people who are willing to step up to His level of thinking and leave the map called, "The known and comfortable." If you dare to be dangerous for Him, then this chapter is for you.

Do you have a dream on the inside you? Then it's time for action. Time to step away from "average" and get busy doing what's in your heart.

BIRTH THE DREAM

What exactly is a dream? I like to define it this way: An inspiring picture of the future that energizes your spirit, soul, and body, empowering you to do everything in your power to achieve it.

B.B.: Dreams are designed to change things.

Martin Luther King, Jr's, famous speech, "I Have A Dream," was all about change—politically, socially, economically, and spiritually. By the way, did you know that wasn't the speech he had planned to give? With input from advisers, King's speech had been composed the night before at Washington's Willard Hotel. As King started to deliver his prepared text, New Orleans' Mahalia Jackson, one of the world's greatest gospel singers, shouted out to him, "Tell them about the dream, Martin. Tell them about the dream!" She obviously ignored the fact that there were almost three hundred thousand other people there that day. King would have probably disregarded anyone else yelling at him, but he didn't ignore Mahalia Jackson.

Clarence Jones, an attorney and adviser to King who had contributed to King's original text, said, "I was standing about fifty feet behind him, to the right and to the rear, and I watched him just take the text of his speech and move it to the left side of the lectern, grab the lectern, look out across the people and begin "I have a dream…""

The rest is history.

The dream in your heart isn't just for you; it's there to make a change for the good of this world and to advance God's Kingdom in the earth.

While dreams come from God, hope is the catalyst that moves you to action. If you don't have hope, you can't be a dreamer. Proverbs 13:12 beautifully states this:

> *"Hope deferred makes the heart sick, but when the desire (dream) comes, it is a tree of life."*

Once you have your dream, there's a process required to turn it into a reality. Of course, we've always heard, "Goals are dreams with a deadline," and in some respects, it's true. I've sat under some of the best goal-setting teachers in the world, even paying a thousand dollars for a day-long session. The information was good, but over the years what I've come to realize is, oftentimes, goals lead to broken focus.

Let me explain.

I've made it a practice not to do pre-marital counseling with couples who have their wedding date set! Why? Because once the date is set, the wedding becomes the goal instead of the marriage. Weddings are for a day; marriages are for a lifetime.

One reason marriages often end prematurely is due to broken focus—too much attention on the wedding date instead of making a life together.

Weddings are fairly easy. Marriages, on the other hand, require much work...for a much longer time period. In the same way, dreams are fairly easy, but fulfilling your dream will cost you...sometimes for a lifetime.

Don't get me wrong; I've set goals and achieved many. Goals are great for short-term pursuits. But for life pursuits, dreams are much more fluid for a few reasons: (1.) you can be led by the Spirit, (2.) your dream can develop and mature over time, and (3.) you can experience the ebb and flow of resources. Take my word for it and do yourself a huge favor. Don't sell yourself short by setting life goals...

...Birth a life dream instead.

BEYOND YOU

One recurring theme in this entire book has been how your life is to be lived for others. Whether it's your perseverance, your commitments, or your willingness to forget, a life lived far above "average" is a life dedicated to blessings others.

Your dream is no exception.

Walt Disney, the founder of the Disney Empire, had a dream to develop a family-friendly theme park based on the characters originated in his animated films. Disneyland in California was the beginning of his dream, but it didn't stop there. Walt Disney World in Orlando, Florida, was the next step.

Although Walt led his company to launch the Florida project, he died before its completion. At the grand opening, a Florida state official said in his speech, "Wouldn't it have been great if Walt would have seen this place?" The next speaker was Walt's wife, Mrs. Lillian Disney. Taking the platform she said, "I'd like to address the comment from the gentleman who was just speaking. Sir, I say this without any unkindness, but if Walt had not seen this, you wouldn't be experiencing it."

That leads me to ask, "Who's waiting to experience your dream?"

Again, your dream is not for you. It's for everyone you've been called to. Your dream becomes somebody else's experience. Because you're willing to see it and pay the price for it today, others will enjoy it tomorrow.

BACK IT UP

While we're talking dreams, visions, plans, and goals, I may be wrong to assume that you have a dream. So let's back up for a moment and address this subject. You can't begin doing a dream until you first have a dream from God.

Let me help you.

First of all, how do you get pregnant with a God-dream? The easiest way I know is to expose yourself to God, His people, and His Kingdom. Secondly, surround yourself with people who are anointed to unlock your purpose—people who believe in you and can empower you. I call them your "permission culture." They're the ones who will create an atmosphere that feels like an experimental laboratory! There, you can take risks and begin to engineer your dream.

God isn't looking for the most qualified people on the planet to carry His dream. No, He's searching for the right heart. Look how 2 Chronicles 16:9 describes it:

"For the eyes of the Lord search back and forth across the whole earth, looking for people whose hearts are perfect toward him, so that he can show his great power in helping them..."

(TLB)

God found a young teenaged girl named Mary and deposited into her a dream to redeem all mankind. That's still His mode of operation today.

B.B.: Big dreams cannot be birthed without a carrier.

Guess what? You're the carrier! But, there's something you need to know.

Just like a woman's ability to become pregnant in the physical can be hindered or even blocked, your dream can be severely hindered or even negated. Your dream needs to be developed in what I call the "safe womb of the Spirit." For this to happen, two things must be addressed:

You must be in right standing with God. I cannot emphasize how crucial this is. Listen, many "dreams" are actually setups by the enemy to take you out. Think about it for a minute. I'm sure you know someone who's on that casualty list. Not even Jesus was immune from this tactic. Right before He was to be released into His global assignment, He was presented several optional "dreams" in the wilderness. What got Him through? His relationship with the Father. The same is true for you.

B.B.: Right relationship with God will birth the right dream.

You may need inner healing. Let me be bold for a moment. I believe about ninety-nine percent of people I've met need inner healing on some level. If you're not familiar with this term, you need to be. It's a practice that depends far less on human capabilities and psychology and more upon the leading of the Holy Spirit. It's not counseling (which can be good); it's a revealing and addressing of inner wounds by the Spirit.

I personally put myself through an inner healing process at least once a year. Unless you live in some Christian "bubble" with no exposure to the world, you're also a prime candidate. How does it work? It's too involved to explain here; however, the Psalmist David laid a great foundation for the process when he cried out to God:

> *"Search me, O God, and know my heart; try me...*
> *And see if there is any wicked way in me..."*

Psalms 139:23-24

You might ask, "Ron, can't I just cry out to God like David did?" Of course you can, and I pray you do on a regular basis. But you're not David! David didn't have Spirit-filled people around to help facilitate him. You do. Find them. Engage with them. Let them help you. You'll be glad you did.

Are you pregnant with a dream? Is it verified by God? Have you received confirmation through an avenue of prayer, prophecy, or straight from God's Word? If yes, then congratulations.

On to the next step: doing.

GOING FULL TERM

When you have a God-birthed dream inside you, the first step towards fulfillment is: You must write it down. If you have already accomplished this step, great! If you haven't, don't go a minute longer without doing it. Do it now. It doesn't have to be detailed at this point. Remember, it's only in a fetus stage right now.

Once you have it written, now you can move on in the process to convert your dream into a reality—the "doing" process.

On the way to maturity, your dream will create a "revelation vacuum" that demands to be filled. In other words, when your dream becomes large enough, it will demand a "how." Don't neglect this stage as it's the blueprint of the entire doing process.

NOTE: Most dreams are aborted at this stage.

Remember the formula: seed...time...harvest. Almost no one wants to wait for their dream to mature. However, your pursuit of the "how" will bring revelation. When your revelation becomes greater than your environment, then your environment can change in the direction of your dream. Once the process begins, just keep repeating it until your dream becomes a reality.

It's on the way!

Have you written down your dream? Have you shown it to someone else? Are you already taking steps toward fulfillment? If you've answered "Yes" to any of these, then let's keep moving forward.

Or, maybe, backward! Yes, sometimes past failures are a part of your dream's fulfillment.

THE WOMB

You've got a dream. You've written it down, received confirmation, and have been highly motivated to walk it out one step at a time. But, something's wrong. Instead of moving forward, it seems you're constantly going backward. Two steps forward, three steps back. Try, try, try, fail. Welcome to the dreamer's life. If this is you, I have some great news for you—maybe the best thing you've read in this entire book. Are you ready?

Failure is the womb of success.

"Ron, how can you say that? You have no idea how many times I've tried and failed." You're right, I don't. But one thing I do know is this: *You'll never move forward until the pain of staying the same is greater than the pain of change.*

Failure isn't final, neither is it fatal…unless you allow it to be. Failure, if you'll let it, can push you towards your dream. If the pain of failure is stopping you dead in your tracks, then you're looking at it all wrong. What's that called again? Broken focus.

Look at David's life. Goliath wasn't David's problem; he was his promotion. The biggest temptations to abort your dream will be during the maturing process. Stay the course! Remember, you have an enemy—a dream stealer—who will use every trick in the book (and then some) to pressure you to give up. Here's what I've come to know:

 B.B.: Your dream will seem the most hopeless right before your greatest breakthrough.

TAKE THE WALK

One of the all-time most quoted stories in the Bible is Peter walking on the water. You know the story. Jesus sent his disciples across the lake and then scared their pants off when He shows up walking on top of the water. Peter then cried out to Jesus, "If that be you bid me to come to you on the water." The rest is history.

As many times as you may have heard this story, I want you to focus in on something that ties into doing your dream. Notice how Peter walking on the water was never Jesus' idea. Jesus didn't ask him or command him. He didn't even suggest it. Peter was the one who had the dream to do something seemingly impossible. God birthed it, Peter dreamed it, and then he presented it to the Son of God for confirmation. What did Jesus say? "Walk on Peter!" The dream was in full motion.

Until the storm took over.

Right in the middle of doing his dream, Peter began to sink. He could've given up and drowned, but Peter did the right thing instead—He looked to Jesus and was saved.

The storms of life will work against your dream in the exact same way. You can't choose when a storm will come, but you can decide what to do while in it. Your storm will do one of three things:

- cause you to hide in the boat.
- try to overtake you during the maturing process.
- cause you to walk on top of what was meant to drown you.

 B.B.: Whatever you do in the storm will determine your accessto your dream.

This one nugget was worth the price of this book!

DO IT

Not only does God birth dreams, He provides the power to do them as well. Let's look at our friend, Walt Disney, once again. He said, "If you can dream it, you can do it." Dreaming is fairly easy. Doing your dream will take God, focus, the help of others, maturity, stick-to-it-iveness, and most of all, faith. Stick with it. It will be worth it in the long haul.

Let your dream be the motivation for your "do." Then, go do it. Walk on that water, baby! Endure what you have to, pay what it takes, refuse to compromise. Don't be "average" and just dream the dream—live above the sea of mediocrity and break through that barrier.

Go and do your dream!

CHAPTER 20

DO MORE THAN LIVE
ONE LIFE...LIVE TWO

I'M GOING TO guess that you probably don't know who Glyndwr Michael is—that is unless you're a student of World History. Allow me to introduce you to this amazing "average buster."

In 1943, Glyndwr Michael—a homeless dead man from London—single handily changed the course of World War II by bringing defeat to Nazi Germany. Here's how it went down.

While the Allies were preparing to invade Nazi-occupied Europe, they discovered that their only marginal access point was Sicily. The problem was that by then, the Nazi regime was so well entrenched and so well armed, passing through Sicily didn't look very hopeful.

That's when Glyndwr Michael came into the picture.

The Allies hatched a plan to pull a dead man from the morgue and change his identity to Major William Martin, a military courier. They then chained a briefcase to his wrist. Inside the briefcase, the British spymasters planted forged documents stating that the target of the invasion was to be Greece. A British submarine then dumped the body of Glyndwr Michael where the Nazi's would find him—making it look like he was a military courier who died in a plane crash.

Amazingly, the plan worked!

The papers were rushed to Hitler who then made the defense of Greece his "top-priority." He dispatched most of his military might headed by the famed General Erwin Rommel. This rouse left Sicily wide open for the European invasion that brought the war to an end the following year.[1]

Glyndwr Michael saved much of the world from the hands of a maniac. How interesting that he did more in his death than what he could never have dreamed of in life.[1]

More than an interesting story, this account parallels this final chapter in this way: To truly defeat the maniac called "average," you must give up your life and live as a dead man with a brand new identity!

The Apostle Paul wrote about this in Galatians 2:20:

> *"I have been crucified with Christ; it is no longer I who live, but Christ lives in me; and the life which I now live in the flesh I live by faith in the Son of God, who loved me and gave Himself for me."*

Did you catch it? "…the life I now live…"

Paul is acknowledging that he used to live one life, but now he's living another. The same applies to you. It's so very important to know that your original life, birthed by your mother, is *not* the only life there is. There is another life—one that is even more original—that God has for you. It starts when you make

Jesus the Lord of your life. It's what Paul meant when he said: "It is no longer I who live, but Christ lives in me..." And, it's also what Jesus was talking about when He said: "I have come that they may have life, and that they may have it more abundantly," (John 10:10).

That, my friend, is the "breaking the barrier of average, more abundant life!" And it's only found one place: in Jesus Christ.

 B.B.: Jesus is the barrier breaker.

Through Jesus, you receive a new and more abundant life. Why would you continue living an old, un-abundant life, when a brand new all-abundant life is waiting? My prayer is that you will embrace the truths in this book, but none of them mean a hill of beans until you lay your life down and receive Jesus as your Lord and Savior. That one act of surrender surpasses all that's written in these chapters, a thousand times over!

CHANGE YOUR LIFE

Have you ever driven a turbocharged car? If not, you should stop at a dealership and ask to drive one. Your life will never be the same. Donna and I have owned several. Here's what happens with a turbo-charged engine.

You begin accelerating like normal, but if you press your foot on the accelerator long enough, the turbo kicks in. BOOM! You're gone!

We owned a little ninety-three horsepower Jetta diesel. The

ironic thing was at this time I had a one-hundred and forty horsepower motorcycle. That was forty-seven more horsepower than Donna's entire care. But let me tell you, when that turbo kicked in, that car ran like a scared rabbit.

It's the same way when you trade your life for the supercharged, turbo life of Jesus. Immediately, you have more joy, more purpose, more love, experience more favor...more of everything good.

Let me encourage you. If you've never laid your life down and picked up the life Jesus offers, don't put it off any longer. You can live more than one life...live two! Not only is your second one better on this earth, it also comes with a promise for eternity.

How do you do this? It's very easy. First, pray and ask Jesus to trade His life for yours. Second, live for Him to the best of your ability.

Number one is easy; number two requires something from you—the laying down of your life. Yes, His life is infinitely better, but dying to yourself can be tough.

But oh so worth it!

If you're ready, pray this prayer and mean it in your heart:

"Dear Jesus, I give you my life and I receive your more abundant life. I thank You for laying down your life on the cross just for me. I now lay my life down for you. Help me, please, to now live your life. In Jesus' name, Amen."

If you prayed that prayer and meant it, I want to be the first to welcome you to the maniac defeating, breaking the barrier of average, more abundant life.

YOUR NEW LIFE

In a horse race, the first place winner usually wins a purse many times the size of the second place horse. Did the first place horse run many times faster? Of course not. Yet, it wins a prize many times greater. So it is with living the far above average life in Christ. With His help and the help of this book, your output may be just three percent above average, but your increase in love, joy, peace, relationships, legacy, faith, and finance will be *many times greater.*

Put this book where you and others will pick it up from time to time and "accidentally" discover some leverage for life. Or, you can pick it up to brush up on some of the areas you need to focus on.

Your best life is waiting for you. Let me say, "Congratulations!" You are now an "average destroyer!"

Now that you're on your second life, I would love to hear more of your journey. Please email me at ron@moreofHim.org.

[1]From the book "The Greatest Stories Never Told" by Rick Beyer)

THE AVERAGE-BUSTER'S CREED

WELCOME TO THE army—the army called "Average Busters!" Like with every military establishment, average busters have a creed to live by. Put this in a place where you can see and speak this over your life every day. In those days where you don't feel so above average (those days will come), pull this out and speak it over and over, until you're convinced you are a destroyer of "average".

The Average Buster Creed:

> I am a soldier in the army of my God.
>
> The Lord Jesus Christ is my commanding officer.
>
> The Holy Bible is my code of conduct.
>
> Faith, prayer and the Word of God are my weapons of warfare.
>
> I have been taught by the Holy Spirit, trained by experience, tried by adversity, and tested by fire.

I am a volunteer in this army, and I am enlisted for eternity.

I will either die in this army or retire at the rapture of the Church.

I will not get out, sell out, be talked out, or be pushed out.

I am faithful, reliable, capable, and dependable.

If my God needs me, I am there—anywhere, any-place, anytime.

I am a soldier.

I am not a baby who needs to be pampered, petted, primed up, pumped up, picked up, or pepped up.

No one has to call me, remind me, write me, visit me, entice me, or lure me.

I am a soldier; I am not a wimp.

I am in my place, saluting my King, obeying His orders, praising His name, and building His Kingdom!

I do not need to be cuddled, cradled, cared for, or catered to.

I am committed.

I cannot have my feelings hurt so badly that I turn around and quit.

I cannot be discouraged enough to turn me aside.

I cannot lose enough to cause me to quit.

If I end up with nothing, I will still come out ahead.

I will win.

My God has, and will continue, to supply all of my needs.

I am more than a conqueror.

I will always triumph.

I can do all things through Christ.

Devils cannot defeat me.

People cannot disillusion me.

Weather cannot weary me.

Sickness cannot stop me.

Battles cannot beat me.

Money cannot buy me.

Governments cannot silence me and hell cannot handle me.

I am a soldier.

Even death cannot destroy me.

When my Commander calls me from this battlefield, He will promote me to Captain and I will rule with Him.

I am a soldier in the army and I'm marching, claiming victory.

I will not give up.

I will not turn around.

I am a soldier marching, heaven bound.

(Author Unknown)

ABOUT THE AUTHOR

RON KUTINSKY IS a man on a mission. As Senior Pastor and Apostolic Leader for H.I.M. Church in Bradenton, Florida, Ron lives to build people of love, destiny, and impact.

Along with pastoring, Ron also serves on the board of several ministries, teaches leadership principles both nationally and abroad, organizes and participates in short-term mission trips, and is an overseer of Gulf Coast School of Supernatural Ministry. He also has a great passion for his family's farm which raises beef cattle on the shores of Berlin lake in Atwater, Ohio.

Ron and his wife Donna live in Parrish, Florida and greatly enjoy the outdoors. Their love for the Kingdom of God is infectious, as shown in their life's creed: "People's success is our honor."

CONTACT RON

Email: ron@moreofHim.org
Facebook: Ron Kutinsky and Hope International Ministries
Book Website: www.breakingthebarrierofaverage.com
Church Website: www.moreofHim.org
Twitter: Ron Kutinsky@revronfl